GOD IS NOT DONE WITH YOU

Walter Albritton

Reid + Carolyn —
May the Lord bless you
with the joy of knowing
you are still in the
Potter's Hands!

Walter Albritton, SJC

Ordering Information:
Copies of this book may be ordered from www.Amazon.com
Or by email from walteralbritton7@gmail.com

God's Not Done With You/Walter Albritton. -- 1st ed.
ISBN 978-1-5403-6626-9

Other Books by Walter Albritton

The Great Secret

When Your Heart is Broken

233 Days
God Hurts Like You Hurt

If You Want to Walk On Water,
You've Got to Get Out of Your Boat

Leaning Over the Banisters of Heaven:
Balcony People Make the Difference

Life is Short
So Laugh Often, Live Fully, and Love Deeply

Just Get Over It And Move On!

Don't Let Go of the Rope!

Walter Albritton had an influence on my life when I was in elementary school in Wetumpka, Alabama. His influence has continued until today. He is a gifted writer. His book is a must-read for anybody who wants to develop a better attitude, a stronger faith, and more wisdom about how to live every day. These essays have come out of a life that has experienced challenges and obstacles, but Walter and Dean have allowed God to help them navigate these issues and turn obstacles into opportunities. He has the capacity to take deep spiritual truths and communicate them in a way that all of us can understand. This is a great book for practical Christian living.

John Ed Mathison
CEO, Leadership Ministries, Montgomery, AL

In the chapter, "Want to Serve God? Then Arm for Battle," you find this arresting statement: "We must find in the strengthening presence of Jesus the courage to stand our ground rather than cut and run." Walter Albritton has stood his ground for Jesus Christ. He has never cut and run and brings to us a practical level of applied courage with his head in the heavens and his feet firmly planted on the ground. This rare gift in words will challenge all of us to refuse to yield and stand our ground for Christ.

Toby Warren, Founder & Chief Servant Officer
National Leadership Congress, God4Vets, Auburn, AL

People who have never met Walter Albritton tell me they eagerly anticipate reading his columns in the local newspaper. This comforting book by a gifted writer, devout man of God and dear friend will be a blessing – it was for me.

Ed Williams
Journalism Professor Emeritus, Auburn University

In these pages Walter shares his life as a follower of Jesus with transparency that will leave you speechless. His powerful, authentic witness, and "Tell it like it is" approach, will compel you to read to the very end. And you will be glad you did!

Ralph Freeman
Song Evangelist, Dunwoody, GA

Having known and worked with Walter Albritton for many years now, I can attest to the fact that Walter has lived out the impactful life lessons that he shares in this inspiring book. In these pages, you will find great wisdom and practical encouragement for your life journey. Walter is a great story teller, and he writes like he preaches - with eloquence and power! Read it, and you will surely know that God is not done with you yet!

Lester Spencer, Lead Pastor
Saint James United Methodist Church, Montgomery, AL

Walter provides a wealth of wisdom and encouragement in this book. He nudges us hopefully toward an everlasting purpose that is larger than time, and helps us hold the hand of the One Who doesn't just point us toward the future, but leads us into it. Read it and soak in the inspiration that springs from it.

Rev. Ron Ball, Executive Director
Academy for Congregational Excellence
Alabama-West Florida Conference, United Methodist Church
Abbeville, AL

God is Not Done With You

by
Walter Albritton

I cannot prove that God exists. I believe he does. I have felt His Presence all of my adult life. My authority for this conviction is the Holy Bible. I do not worship the Bible but I believe it is the single greatest source of truth available to inquiring minds. I like what Martin Luther said – that the Scriptures are the crib in which God has presented his Son to the world. The crib has value but the Son is the great treasure. The Scriptures teach me that God "so loved" the world that he gave us his Son, that believing in him we might not perish but have eternal life.

The Scriptures teach me that Jesus died on the cross for my sins and that God raised him from the dead. The Scriptures teach me that Christ is alive and will live in my heart if I will acknowledge him as my Lord and Savior. The Scriptures teach me that the living Christ has invited me to live in this world as Christ's servant and his witness. The Scriptures teach me that God has commanded me to love him with all my heart and to love others as I love myself.

The Scriptures teach me that while I can do "nothing" in my own strength, God will pour into my life his Holy Spirit who will empower me to accomplish his will for my life. The Scriptures teach me that I am a soul with a body, not a body with a soul, and that reading and inwardly digesting the Holy Scriptures keeps my soul alive and well.

The Scriptures teach me that while I will have heartaches and trials in this world, the living Christ will replace my sorrow with his joy and give me the strength to rise again and again to serve him until my last breath. For more than 60 years I have done my best to live as a servant of Jesus Christ. In this I have failed often but along the way, as a young man, I became aware of this profound truth: God is not done with me until the final curtain is drawn.

Again and again, the Inner Voice has said to me, "Walter, I am not done with you yet. Stop feeling sorry for yourself. Get up and I will help you take the next step on this journey I have planned for you." I cannot find the words to describe the joy in my heart from knowing that the Living God is still working on me! All I can say is Glory!

Whatever your situation in life, I dare you to believe that God is not done with you! Run from self-pity and self-despising. Laugh at your troubles and see in the midst of life's storms that your heavenly Father is still working on you! Clear the runway and give the God who loves you a chance to make you what he wants you to be! As you read these pages, yield to the Potter who is able to shape you into the beautiful person he wants you to be!

Thank you for allowing me the honor of sharing my heart with you. I pray that the Lord will speak to you through the words which I offer in His Name.

Walter Albritton, sjc
Servant of Jesus Christ

The Cabin
Wetumpka, Alabama
December, 2016

CONTENTS

CHAPTER ONE

He's Still Working On Me

Grieving in a deep, dark hole of disillusionment?
Sick of glib comments from people who don't understand
   your pain?
Tired of other people telling you how you should feel?
Depressed because God did not answer your prayers?
Heartbroken and feeling like a failure?
Feel like a broken pot that God is ready to discard?
About ready to give up on God?
Thinking God may have given up on you?
Miserable because life does not make sense?
Angry because your dreams have been crushed?

If any of those feelings are yours, then I am so glad you picked up this book. At one time or another I have had all of those feelings. I want to share with you what I have learned from a lifetime of struggling with all these issues.

As you reflect on my observations, consider what God may be saying to you through the honest feelings of a fellow struggler. God teaches us through the experiences of others. I have benefitted much from observing and listening to others. My prayer is that

God will give you a glimmer of hope, a word of encouragement or cheer, or a reason to keep going as I share my heart with you in the pages that follow. My thoughts are not deep and mysterious but hopefully they are not shallow. They are the best insights God has given me about the basic issues of life. Try to imagine that we are sitting together in glider chairs on a front porch in a place you love, just sharing our hearts with each other. I hope you will find my writing conversational.

I will begin with the heartbreaking death of our son at age 3. When David died I thought my life was over. I was only 24 and in seminary at Vanderbilt University studying to become a pastor. That semester one of my subjects was "Systematic Theology." It was all about the Christian doctrine of the nature of God but I had no good news to share with people about God. God had let my son die with leukemia. He had turned a deaf ear to my agonizing prayers for our son's healing. Who would believe me if I told them what the Bible says, that God is love? No church would want a preacher who was heartbroken and confused about God. My wife would have no reason to support my ministry. If I asked her to trust God and share ministry with me, she would give me a blank stare and say, "Oh sure, that sounds like an exciting life – serving a God who lets little children die." We were in a dark tunnel spiritually and I could see no light at the end.

The next few years were filled with more grief than joy. Life did go on but it was a grind. We tried to put on glad faces and move forward despite our pain. Gradually I discovered that God had not given up on me, though I thought many times about giving up on him. I had to admit that God seemed to be giving me the strength to pick up the pieces and go on living despite the death of our only child. Though I was not conscious of it at the time, I recognized as I looked back that God was still working on me.

That became a profound insight: God was not done with me. That I was still alive was God's will. I began to see that in all the circumstances of my life, God was using my problems to sand off my rough edges. I was like clay in the hands of a potter. I was a miserable, broken pot but he had not thrown me away in disgust. So if God had hope for me, I could have some hope for myself. That small hope began to grow as I felt his hands shaping and working on me.

As the years rolled on my wife gave birth to four more fine sons. We had a family. We were a family. We felt the Potter at work in those days, shaping us into the kind of parents we needed to be. Our grief was not always on the front burner. We were not "getting over" David's death but we were getting "beyond" it.

Then, in our early forties our marriage began to disintegrate. Marital conflict led me to see that I was obsessed with my ministry as an evangelist and blind to the neglect of my family. Wanting to put first things first, I resigned from my evangelism position and returned to pastoral ministry. My sons, and my wife, needed me at home and my work as a pastor would make me a resident daddy. My wife welcomed this change and our marriage began slowly healing. Both of us were encouraged by the feeling that God was still working on us. We knew we had a long way to go but it felt good to believe that we were still clay in the Potter's hands and that he was not done with us.

As our boys grew up the pressures of parenting and pastoral ministry created more stress than I could handle. Flat on my back in a hospital, diagnosed with a bleeding ulcer and 45 years old, I was one miserable human being. I was a wreck. One minute I was scared I was going to die; the next minute I wanted to die. My life was over. I was a failure as a father and as a pastor. My congregation would have no confidence in a sick preacher whose sons were being arrested for public drinking and raising hell. But one more time the Potter refused to throw me on the trash heap of broken pottery.

Once again I felt his hands upon me, molding and shaping me into a vessel he could use. One more time my sense of unworthiness was overcome by the reality that God was still working on me. To my miserable, broken spirit God whispered, "I am not done with you yet." As I slowly regained my health, I found new confidence in my gifts for ministry and saw signs that God was restoring my joy in serving him. For a few years all was going well.

Then I hit the wall again. Accepted and well received in most of the churches I served, I was appointed to one that was not a good fit. Conflict with the power brokers of the church led to my being reassigned to another church after two years. This time, more than ever before, I struggled with self-despising, depression and self-pity but the Lord rescued me again. Despite my mistakes and poor judgment, God had mercy on me. Leaders of my next church affirmed me, restoring my confidence that I could serve effectively as a pastor. Once again I was overwhelmed by the awareness that the God who created the heavens and the earth was still working on me. He was not done with me!

At age 70 the mandatory retirement age rule of the United Methodist Church made it necessary for me to retire. When the time came for me to say goodbye to the dear people I had served for 13 years, I was a basket case. My life was over. We moved from Opelika to Elmore County, back home near the place where I was born.

Miserable spiritually, I was also a wreck physically, so crippled in both knees that I could hardly walk. My orthopedic surgeon and dear friend Dr. Jim Whatley scheduled surgery. When he explained that both knees were equally bad, and asked me to choose the one to be replaced, I asked if he could replace both knees at the same time. He said he could so I said, "Do it." That was not one of my brightest decisions; the next day I did not have a leg to stand on! To make matters even worse, blood clots developed without warning and the good doctor said after several panic-stricken hours, "We almost lost you."

I did recover but a funny thing happened before I was discharged from the hospital. My friend Lester Spencer, then pastor of Saint James United Methodist Church in Montgomery, came to see me. In the hospital where two days before I had almost died from blood clots, Lester invited me to come on staff at Saint James. I laughed at his proposal but told him that if I could find a way to walk again, I would be honored to join his team.

After Lester left my room, that jarring thought of times past hit me again: God is not done with you! A few hours before I had been knocking on death's door. But now, helpless in a hospital bed and unable to walk, I laughed out loud – the Creator and Redeemer of the world was still working on me! While weeks of severe depression were just ahead, it would be that idea that restored my confidence to resume pastoral ministry. It remains a GLORY MOMENT for me.

God's kindness has afforded me 13 years of ministry with the Saint James church family. Deep, abiding friendships with many strong disciples of Christ have developed. I have had the honor of preaching the good news of Jesus almost every Sunday. I have shared the sorrow of those whose loved ones have run ahead of us to the Father's House. I have united some fifty couples in holy matrimony. I have baptized two dozen infants, several young people and quite a number of adults. I have spent many hours counseling troubled souls to find the faith and energy to get up and get back in the game of life.

Along the way the strength of my body has declined as expected in the aging process. Medicine that saved me from pneumonia severely affected the tendons of my ankles and feet, leaving me with balance difficulty in walking. Physical therapy and a walking stick have become necessary.

I think about death now much more than when I was young. At age 84 I realize I am around third base and getting ready to slide across home plate. I don't dread dying. I am not afraid to die. Yet I do wonder how and when the end will come for me. Will it be a heart attack, a stroke, cancer or an accident? While I choose not to worry about my departure I find it impossible not to wonder how it will happen. But I find comfort by leaving the matter in the Father's hands.

Pondering my death is not depressing. The fact that I am still alive reminds me that God is not done with me yet. That excites me. That encourages me to ponder important questions. For example, what does God expect of me in these days of my life? For most of my adult life I have known that God wants to make me more like Christ. Since that work is not done yet, I need to surrender more fully to his power to transform my poor character into the character of Christ.

I love the children's song titled "He's Still Working On Me" written by Joel Hemphill. Its theology fits my experience of God perfectly!

He's still working on me
To make me what I need to be
It took him just a week to make the moon and stars,
The sun and the earth and Jupiter and Mars.
How loving and patient He must be,
He's still working on me

There really ought to be a sign upon the heart,
Don't judge her yet, there's an unfinished part.

But I'll be perfect just according to His plan
Fashioned by the Master's loving hands.

In the mirror of His Word reflections that I see
Make me wonder why He never gave up on me.
He loves me as I am and helps me when I pray
Remember He's the Potter, I'm the clay.

Now you know the song that has inspired me for years to cherish the truth that God is still working on me, patiently making me what he wants me to be, and inviting me to remember each day to be like clay in the hands of the Master Potter.

When God called me to preach at age 18 I ran like Jonah only instead of heading to Tarshish, I headed to Auburn University. There I soon had a job working in the press box so I hid out there for a while. I had thoughts of becoming a sports writer or an English teacher. But the Lord found me, called me out of that press box and told me he had another plan. He was indeed loving and patient; he kept working on me until one day I was pastor of five churches on the LaPlace Charge. I did not know how to write a sermon, much less how to preach. I had zero training about how to be a pastor. So when I got a chance to go to seminary I jumped at the chance and was soon as Vanderbilt Divinity School in Nashville.

Our son's death robbed Dean and me of any "marital bliss" we may have had and wounded our relationship. We handled grief differently. And while I became a pastor after seminary, and God blessed us with four more sons, Dean and I were not a team in ministry. Far from it. When I tried to get Dean to help me with church stuff, she said bluntly, "God didn't call me to preach.

I have all I can do to take care of these boys." So I blundered on, frustrated and struggling, doing ministry in my own strength.

Then one day we stumbled into something wonderful. At a retreat called an Ashram we came under the vibrant influence of E. Stanley Jones, a missionary and evangelist. Desperate and hungry for an authentic relationship to God, on our knees we surrendered our lives to the Holy Spirit. I still do not know how to explain it but we were changed. Nothing dramatic occurred. We heard no angels singing but we experienced power that was new to us. We discovered firsthand how the Lord "makes all things new." The grass was greener. The sky was bluer. We were free in ways we never dreamed possible. By the grace of God, we became a team and to this day we are still having fun being a team, working together as servants of Jesus.

Dean and I are so thankful for the Lord's patience with us and thrilled that he is "still working on us to make us what we need to be." We both realize that we are Christians in the making; the Lord is still making us what he wants us to be. And we praise God that he is not done with us yet!

We should not be surprised that the Lord is not done with us, two old people who have been in ministry for 65 years. After all the Bible tells marvelous stories of how God delighted in "working on" old people. Take Abraham, for example. He was 75 when the Lord called him to pack up and leave Haran and go to an unknown place. Years went by and when Abraham was 100 and Sarah was 90, God surprised them with a baby boy named Isaac.

Some years later God tested Abraham by asking him to offer his beloved son Isaac on the altar. At the last minute God stopped him from killing his son and provided instead a ram caught in a thicket. I can imagine Abraham wiping his brow later and saying to Sarah, "He's still working on me."

When famine hit Canaan, Abraham sold his wife to the Pharaoh in Egypt, passing her off as his sister. God was patient with Abraham's lying ways. Sarah may well have said to Abraham, "How patient and kind God has been with you!"

Despite all the problems Abraham had with Hagar and Ishmael, God kept working on him so that he could fulfill the covenant to make Abraham a blessing and a father to many nations. He finally died at the age of 175, "an old man and full of years." You can only imagine how many times over all those years that Abraham may have rejoiced in the truth that God was not done with him!

God's patience with Abraham shows us the true nature of God. Patiently he keeps working on us to make us like Christ, for that is what he wants us to be. The blind hymn writer George Matheson expressed this truth in his song, "O Love that Will Not Let Me Go.' In spite of our failures and fumbles, God will not stop loving us.

To experience the life-changing power of God we must each become willing for him to change us. God does not force his way into our lives. He waits, patiently, for us to become tired of the status quo and say, "Jesus, I want you to work on me. I want you to make me what you want me to be."

You have a choice. You can continue being an observer or you can get in the game. No matter what problems you have now, what mountains you are trying to climb, as long as you have breath, God is not done with you yet! He wants to work on you but he waits for you to become willing to be clay in his hands. He waits for you to ask him to mold you and shape you into what he wants you to be.

We Methodists love to sing an historic Wesleyan hymn, "And Are We Yet Alive." Charles Wesley wrote it for the Methodists to sing as they gathered for their annual meetings. Mull over the words: "And are we yet alive, and see each other's face? Glory and thanks to Jesus give for his almighty grace!" Many of the early circuit riders in America died before age 35. So being alive was exciting to them; they did not have cell phones for instant communication and were thrilled to find that some of their friends were still alive.

One famous circuit rider back in the 1800s was Peter Cartwright. He was a passionate preacher of the gospel. In his old age he reminisced about earlier days when many times he had to camp out in the woods without fire or food for himself or his horse. He said, "We murdered the King's English and our library consisted of little more than a Bible and a hymnbook, but we preached the gospel with unction and the power of God fell upon thousands who turned to Jesus for salvation." I can imagine Cartwright camping out in the woods and saying to his horse, "Partner, the good Lord is not done with us yet!"

Ponder that phrase: "And are we yet alive." You are alive, but how alive are you? Do you have victory in Jesus? Do you have the inner joy of knowing that Jesus has saved you from your sins? Have you experienced deliverance from the bondage of evil addictions? Have you a passionate desire to share Jesus with others so that friends and family members still in bondage may be delivered by the power of God?

Do you find yourself often praising God for your blessings and your salvation? Is your heart filled with gratitude for what the Lord has done for you? Do you feel like praising God that he is not done with you? Does your heart rejoice that he is still working on you?

Here is the big question: Are you willing to turn to Jesus and say to him with all your heart, "Jesus I want to repent of being satisfied with a life without passion or joy, and I want to surrender to you in a new way. I want you to keep working on me to make me what you want me to be. I give you permission to use my pain, my failures, my sins, to make me the person you want me to be. I want you to do a new work of grace in me so that when I come to worship you on Sunday I will rejoice to see the faces of my friends and be eager to say with them, 'Glory and thanks to Jesus give for his almighty grace'!"

I covet for you, until your last breath, the joyous awareness that God is still patiently working on you! May you arise each new day until he calls you home and celebrate with great joy this amazing truth: God is not done with you! Glory! +

CHAPTER 2

Folks Who Refuse to Give Up

Trouble reveals our true character. When trouble comes, some folks cut and run. Others refuse to give up. These tough people are the ones we admire. They are our heroes – the people who refuse to quit in the face of adversity.

I have known and admired several such people. One was Johnnie Johnston. She was 88 when I met her. Johnnie was a painter. She gave me one of her oil paintings of an open Bible on a pulpit. She said, "I painted that one when I was 85. I had to paint it with my left hand because my right hand had been paralyzed by a stroke."

I never heard Johnnie complain. She stayed busy painting, cooking and doing things for other people. She had no time to feel sorry for herself. People needed her so like her Lord she "went about doing good."

Stella Bush was another. The first time I saw her was the Sunday someone brought her into church in a wheelchair. I found out she was paralyzed from the neck down. But she could still talk.

That Sunday she told me God told her to come to church and give her heart to Jesus.

The next day she called me and asked me if there was anything she could do for the Lord. She told me her caretaker dialed my number and held the phone so she could talk to me. So every Monday I gave her a few names and numbers of people who had missed church the previous day. You can imagine the shock people got when a paralyzed woman called to say "We missed you in church yesterday."

Joe Hamilton was another hero. He was homebound; diabetes had robbed him of a leg but he did not whine about it. Instead he was cheerful and talked about former days when he was healthy.

When his doctor advised Joe he would have to lose his other leg, Joe said to me, "I will be all right; I still have both arms." And he was all right. He asked for no sympathy and refused to feel sorry for himself. Joe's remarkable courage showed me how God can help a man face devastating trouble without fear or flinching.

Maude Smith was a widow. She lived alone but she was not a bitter recluse. If she was ever depressed, she never let on. Whenever Maude was around, people were smiling and laughing. She was a carrier of good cheer.

Many women crochet; Maude baked cakes. She did not wait for birthdays. She baked cakes and gave them to people just for the joy of doing it. Her cakes, and her cheerful countenance, made you aware that loneliness can be overcome by caring for others.

John Jones was diagnosed with cancer. He had to retire early. Cancer and the treatment for it robbed him of energy, denying him many of the privileges he once enjoyed. But he chose to be better, not bitter. His family said he never complained right up to the time of his final illness.

He saw death coming down the road looking for him. He refused to give up and go quietly. As long as he had breath, he lived every day to the fullest. John looked death in the face and said, "You cannot take my life because I have already given it to God. My future is in his hands, not yours."

My friend Ben was hospitalized in February. Risky heart surgery was recommended though the doctors warned he might not survive it. The surgery was successful but slowly it became obvious he was not going to recover. Once or twice we thought he was dying but he revived. He said he saw "the light" and was not afraid. He told us he was at peace and had no fear of dying. Weeks later he crossed over to the other side without fear. While he was still lucid I had thanked him for our 60-year friendship and we laughed about being together again soon. He was my age. His last gift was showing me how to die peacefully without fear.

When it comes my time to slip through that thin curtain that separates this life from the next, I want to do so like Ben did, without fear. That would be one small way of paying my debt to those remarkable people who stayed the course and kept the faith when hard times came their way. +

CHAPTER 3

Just Get Over It and Move On

Disappointments happen. We stumble. We fall. We get our feelings hurt. Friends let us down. We shoot ourselves in the foot.

In miserable moments we experience anger, frustration and despair. We kick ourselves. We should have done better. We may even want to die. A cloud of gloom hangs over us. We are embarrassed. We want to run and hide and never look another person in the face.

Weary of this misery we finally decide we have punished ourselves enough. Life is difficult. The past cannot be undone. We must work our way through these wretched feelings and start living again. What works for me is to walk away from the mess I have made and start over.

Just get over it and move on! Worry changes nothing. Bitterness sours the spirit. Regret must quickly give way to change. Face reality. Admit it if I have been at fault. Ask forgiveness if I have offended someone. Take responsibility for my actions.

If I have done or said something stupid, I can make amends. I can try again. I can become a more sensitive, caring person. I can offer others the support and encouragement I wish they would offer me.

The death of a loved one can result in heartbreaking disappointment. We experience sorrow but also remorse about what we may have failed to do. Remorse can lead to debilitating depression. While grief is normal we must eventually get over it. Life does not stand still; it moves on. Sadness must give way to joy.

In dark days we look for light where we can find it. The words of Thomas Carlyle are helpful: "The eternal stars shine out as soon as it is dark enough." If we will gaze up into the dark sky long enough, we will soon see the stars shining. They are there, waiting to be seen, but it is hard to see them through our tears.

Life is not all sunshine and sweetness. There are sad and lonely days, but we have a choice; we can choose to get beyond our misery. Henry Wadsworth Longfellow understood this reality:

Be still, sad heart, and cease repining,
Behind the clouds the sun is shining;
Thy fate is the common fate of all;
Into each life some rain must fall, --
Some days must be dark and dreary.

Adversity is a great teacher. We learn more from our failure than our success. Success often leads to pride and pride causes us to stumble. When we fall, we need to ask what caused us to fall and resolve to improve wherever possible. Only a fool continues to make the same mistake repeatedly. We can learn not to do certain things again. Unless we do, we will never be able to "get over it."

Some people get ahead by stepping on others on the way to the top. It hurts when someone gets the promotion you thought you deserved. When that happens, you have a choice. You can stew over it and complain bitterly. You can scream and cry that you were wronged. None of that will help. It succeeds only in making you miserable. The best response you can make? Just grab yourself by the nap of the neck and get over it.

To get over a disappointment is to rise above it. Washington Irving said it well: "Little minds are tamed and subdued by misfortune; but great minds rise above it." He was right. We can refuse to be subdued by our defeats and become better people because of them.

Anger is self-destructive. Problems are never solved by tearing our hair out. Baldness will not soothe our sorrows. Though it is normal to become angry with those who hurt us, we can learn to calm down and get over the hurt.

Forgiveness is better than anger. Hatred is a chain that ties you to the person you hate. The only way to be free is to forgive. Forgiveness breaks the chain and sets you free.

If you are nursing a sorrow, hurt, disappointment or failure, admit that you need to get over it. If you get over it, you can move on with your life. Life will not be perfect, but it will be sweeter, and you will be able to share with your friends: "I'm over it!"

The next time life falls apart for you, do yourself a big favor. Skip the misery of disappointment and regret. Just get over it and move on! +

CHAPTER 4

Get Up and Get Back in the Game!

People who refuse to quit inspire the rest of us to try again when we have failed. I never tire of reading stories about people who had the guts to get back in the game after being knocked down.

Tim Tebow, for example, failed in his dream of becoming a quarterback in the NFL. At age 29 Tebow began working hard to realize a new dream: become a major league baseball player.

Critics said Tebow was too slow. Others, like former major league catcher Chad Moeller, believed Tim could make it.

Whether or not Tebow achieves his new dream, you just have to admire him for the effort. I am cheering for him to make it.

I don't know Hue Jackson, the new coach of the Cleveland Browns, but I like his attitude. Jackson refuses to believe the Browns cannot have a winning season.

Jackson says, "We are going to work as hard as anybody so I think we stand as good a chance as anybody to win. We are not going to sit here and say uncle. It's just not who we are. And I'll never be that way." I love his spirit.

After a poor performance in trials, Gabby Douglas was not expected to make the five-woman U.S. Olympic gymnastics team. In tryouts Gabby fell twice from the balance beam. But Coach Marta Karolyi chose Gabby for the team anyway because of her reputation as a fighter who excels under pressure.

In Rio Gabby proved worthy of Karolyi's trust by performing brilliantly as the U.S. team won Olympic gold once again. Gabby got up and dusted herself off and got back in the game!

E. Stanley Jones traveled the world as an evangelist and missionary. I was blessed to hear him speak many times. He often explained that what kept him going in his later years was grace and gumption. By gumption he meant the resilience to get up and get back in the game.

When Jones was 88 he suffered a stroke that seriously impaired him physically but not mentally and spiritually. Though severely impaired in his speech, he dictated one final book titled *The Divine Yes* and even managed to preach several times from his wheelchair.

In so doing Jones practiced what he preached and his example inspired many others to believe that, with a little grace and gumption, they could get up and get back in the game.

Consider this possibility: the next time you get knocked down, if you refuse to stay down, you could get up and get back in the game – and inspire someone else to follow your example. All the grace you need is available – but you have to provide the gumption. +

CHAPTER 5

While It is Day, Take Care of Business

John tells in his gospel about Jesus meeting a blind man, then teaching his disciples a lesson about life. Jesus says, "We must do the work of him who sent me while it is day." He went on to say that the night is coming when no one can work.

My dad, who had an amazing work ethic, used to say after a brief break from work on the farm, "Boys, we are burning daylight; let's get to work!" He insisted on working until the sun went down.

Philosopher Elton Trueblood borrowed the phrase, "While It Is Day," from Jesus and used it as the title of his autobiography, his final book. He was 74 at the time and would live another 20 years but felt it wise to sum up his life "while it was day."

The lesson here is that it is wise for us, no matter our age, to take care of business while the sun is shining since none of us knows what a day may bring forth. We do know that one day the night will come and our working days will be over.

Opportunities come. Opportunities pass. Opportunities are lost. Wise we are to take advantage of every opportunity that comes our way – and not burn daylight doing it.

Malcolm Muggeridge was a journalist – and an agnostic. He became a Christian after an interview with Mother Teresa. Toward the end of his life he wrote a book titled "Confessions of a 20th Century Pilgrim." Reflecting on the prospect of his death, he said he was not troubled about what he had done wrong, the sins he wished he had not done. He was haunted, he said, about his failure to earnestly seize the opportunities God had given him.

Researchers at Cornell University did a survey to find out what people regretted the most. They found that twice as many people were bothered more by what they did not do than what they had done. Missed opportunities were at the top of the list of all regrets. Most regrets were from those who were afraid to take a chance and risk failure.

Television has popularized the phrase, "prime time." Certain hours of the day are "prime time." When it comes to matters of eternal significance, it seems fair to say that now, this very moment, is prime time to respond to doors God has opened, to opportunities that may be lost if we dillydally around and burn daylight.

Pastor Ron Buford tells of his mother having Alzheimer's. She was in a nursing home and had not recognized Ron for months. Even so he went by for a brief visit every morning. One day she recognized him immediately and joyfully called his name. Ron said, "I canceled my other plans for that morning, knowing two things: this moment may never come again, and it did not, and I knew that no one ever again might be that happy to see me." He says, "I still remember those moments as if they happened yesterday."

Whatever your situation, you will be wise to take care of business while it is day. +

CHAPTER 6

Worry Robs Life of Joy and Balance

Pneumonia stopped me in my tracks. Put me in the hospital. Got me to thinking about dying. But that is not bad. Everybody, young or old, needs to do some serious thinking about death because each of us is going to die.

One thing I am not going to do is worry about my death. Worry can kill you. I may not be able to stop pneumonia from killing me but I have a choice about worry. I can stop worry in its tracks by refusing to worry. Unchecked, worry will rob my life of joy and balance. I can choose to not allow that robbery to take place.

Nobody recommends worrying. In fact, everybody frowns on doing it. To reinforce my decision not to worry, I decided to collect ten good quotations about the danger and futility of worrying.

Corrie ten Boom said, "Worry does not empty tomorrow of its sorrow, it empties today of its strength."

Charlie Brown said, "I've developed a new philosophy.... I only dread one day at a time."

Pat Schroeder said, "You can't wring your hands and roll up your sleeves at the same time."

Thomas Edison said, "As a cure for worrying, work is better than whiskey."

Douglas MacArthur said, "Worry, doubt, fear and despair are the enemies which slowly bring us down to the ground and turn us to dust before we die."

Tim Fargo said, "Worry trades the joy of now for the un-likely catastrophes of later."

William Ralph Inge said, "Worry is interest paid on trouble before it comes due."

Robert Eliot said, "Rule number one is, don't sweat the small stuff. Rule number two is, it's all small stuff."

Mary C. Crowley said, "Every evening I turn my worries over to God. He's going to be up all night anyway."

Number ten will, as you might expect, be these words of Jesus as they are paraphrased by Eugene Peterson in *The Message*: *"If God gives such attention to the appearance of wildflowers—most of which are never even seen—don't you think he'll attend to you, take pride in you, do his best for you? What I'm trying to do here is to get you to relax, to not be so preoccupied with getting, so you can respond to God's giving. People who don't know God and the way he works fuss over these things, but you know both God and how he works. Steep your life in God-reality, God-initiative, God-provisions. Don't worry about missing out. You'll find all your everyday human concerns will be met.*

"Give your entire attention to what God is doing right now, and don't get worked up about what may or may not happen tomorrow. God will help you deal with whatever hard things come up when the time comes." (Matthew 6:30-34)

I like that idea that we should pay attention to what God is doing right now rather than worry about tomorrow. So when worry knocks on my door, I tell it to go away because I am focused on how I can participate in what God is doing – and God is always up to something good!

Life in this world is a gift – and I intend to enjoy it to the full as long as God gives me breath. When I turned my life over to Jesus he gave me another precious gift – the gift of eternal life. Eternal life begins in this life and continues beyond death in the place God has prepared for those who love him. There in the presence of the one who died for my sins, I shall praise God with a new voice in a new body forever thanking him for the amazing grace that saved a wretch like me.

Whether I live another ten days or ten years need not concern me. I shall thank God for each new sunrise. Worry will not lengthen my days. Nothing is gained by worrying about things over which I have no control. I am in the Lord's hands – here and there. Therefore, I shall not worry but trust him in all things small and great. Step aside and let me put my hand to the plow while it is day! Glory Hallelujah! +

CHAPTER 7

Make Today Count

I picked up an old book one day, began thumbing through it and got blessed. The book was written by Elisabeth Kubler-Ross titled *Death – The Final Stage of Growth*, published in 1975.

The word "death" got my attention. In recent days death has claimed three dear friends so death and dying have been on my mind. And with each passing of a friend, I am reminded that my days are also numbered.

The book is helpful but the source of my blessing was something written by a friend of Kubler-Ross. The friend was Orville Kelly who, in his forties, became terminally ill with cancer. In the midst of his suffering Kelly started an organization called "Make Today Count." Kelly's purpose was to allow terminally ill patients to share and help each other combat loneliness and isolation. The organization continues long after Kelly's death to make a difference nationwide.

A dying man who wanted to live but knew he had to bid adieu to his loved ones, Kelly shared his feelings in a poem which he gave as a gift to Kubler-Ross. It was titled "For my Wife,

Wanda: Love Will Never Go Away." It was first published in Kubler-Ross's book on death.

As I contemplate my own passing, I wish I could express my feelings with half the beauty of Kelly's stirring words. So now I share my blessing, what I consider one of the most beautiful poems ever written:

Spring, and the land lies fresh green
Beneath a yellow sun.
We walked the land together, you and I
And never knew what future days would bring.
Will you often think of me,
When flowers burst forth each year?
When the earth begins to grow again?
Some say death is so final,
But my love for you can never die.
Just as the sun once warmed our hearts
Let this love touch you some night,
When I am gone,
And loneliness comes –
Before the dawn begins to scatter
Your dreams away.

Summer, and I never knew a bird
Could sing so sweet and clear,
Until they told me I must leave you
For a while.
I never knew the sky could be so deep a blue,
Until I knew I could not grow old with you
But better to be loved by you,
Than to have lived a million summers,
And never known your love.

Together, let us, you and I
Remember the days and nights,
For eternity.

Fall, and the earth begins to die,
And leaves turn golden-brown upon the trees.
Remember me, too, in autumn, for I will walk with you,
As of old, along a city sidewalk at evening-time,
Though I cannot hold you by the hand.

Winter, and perhaps someday there may be
Another fireplace, another room,
With crackling fire and fragrant smoke,
And turning, suddenly, we will be together,
And I will hear your laughter and touch your face,
And hold you close to me again.
But, until then, if loneliness should seek you out,
Some winter night, when snow is falling down,
Remember, though death has come to me,
Love will never go away!

In this touching poem Orville Kelly shared some of the deep feelings I wish I could express to the marvelous woman who has graced my journey for almost 65 years. +

CHAPTER 8

If You Will Hold My Hand

I had no idea it was after midnight until I glanced at my watch. For several hours I had been engaged in an intense conversation with a friend who insisted he was "a Judas" because he did not believe in God. He was an officer in our church, one of our trusted leaders.

At his invitation I had stopped by earlier that evening for a chat. Almost immediately he had said, "I feel like Judas because I don't believe there is a God." His confession shocked me so I took on the challenge to persuade him he was wrong.

Our conversation was not heated. He said he wanted to believe and hoped I could help him overcome his skepticism. But no matter what I said, he remained unconvinced. Wearily, with a look of utter sadness, he said, "I think I am an atheist, and worse than that because for years I have pretended to be a Christian."

Weary myself, and feeling defeated, I could think of nothing more to say. Feebly I expressed the hope that I had been of some help to him and asked if I might offer a prayer before we parted.

His response pierced my heart like an arrow. Calmly he said, "You can pray if you want to but I don't think there is anybody out there listening." I prayed anyway and left for home quite discouraged.

I wish I could report that sometime later my friend chose to have faith in God. But alas, I cannot. I do not know if he ever chose to believe in God. We never discussed the matter again. I was shortly in another town and another man was his pastor. Years have come and gone and I have often wondered if he ever got to know the living God.

Many people find it difficult to believe there is a God who cares about each of us. There are seven billion people in the world. The idea of a loving God who cares about each of is mind-boggling. And if you accept the idea that God loves us, you must then explain why he allows bad things to happen to us.

Difficult questions remind us that most religions, including Christianity, involve faith. And while there are many ways to define faith, most would agree that faith is believing in something for which there is no visible proof. So to believe God exists requires faith.

At age four our youngest son Steve insisted that he did not need major surgery on his chest. The doctor insisted that without the surgery Steve would soon be dead. Finally, Steve surrendered to the inevitable and said, "Daddy, I can do it if you hold my hand." I held his hand tightly until the anesthesiologist had put him to sleep. When he awakened hours later I was holding his hand.

Believing in God is like trying to hold the hand of someone you cannot see. It is a biblical figure of speech that is also imbedded in the songs of the church.

Just before Jesus died, he said from the cross, "Father, into thy hands I commit my spirit" (Luke 23:46). And I love what God said to his servant Isaiah, "So do not fear, for I am with you; do not be dismayed, for I am your God. I will strengthen you and help you; I will uphold you with my righteous right hand" (Isaiah 41:10).

Jesus knew that God is a spirit and that spirits do not have hands. But still our faith is buoyed by simple songs we learned as children, such as "He holds the whole world in his hands; he holds me and you brother in his hands." To speak of the hands of God is to use a metaphor that expresses faith.

When my sister Laurida was dying I held her hand as I stood beside her hospital bed. At her funeral I choked up trying to sing the poignant song, "Precious Lord, take my hand." There is a phrase in that song that expresses the cry of every heart, *"When my life is almost gone, hear my cry, hear my call, hold my hand lest I fall; take my hand, precious Lord, lead me home."*

I hope my friend who felt like Judas finally decided to ask God to hold his hand. Perhaps, on a Sunday in some spring, he realized that Easter is God's gift of hope and took the hand of the risen Christ. If so, he is now enjoying that greater life that awaits believers on the other side.

Until then we who are still here can look death in the face and fearlessly proclaim the best news the world has ever received: Christ is Risen! He is Risen indeed! +

CHAPTER 9

Turning your Home Over to God

In the spring of 1960 my wife Dean and I built a small concrete-block house in Elmore County not far from Wetumpka, Alabama. It was our hideaway in the woods, a place of retreat from parsonage life. We called it "The Cabin."

Our little house grew from 600 square feet to its current size, about 3,000 square feet. Our son Steve, who moved from studying biology to building homes, added a spacious "great room" just before we retired. With a high ceiling and a fireplace, the room is larger than the original house. I enjoy telling people we have a beautiful room with a cabin on the back.

Dean suggested we dedicate the room to the Lord and invite others to use it. We did that and sharing the room with others has brought us great joy. Family members have used it for small group meetings. One church used it for an all-day staff planning retreat. We have used the room for sewing groups, prayer meetings, suppers, birthday parties and Bible study.

Turning one's home over to God is not a new idea. The church began in homes. New churches usually begin in a home. In countries like China today there are thousands of "house" churches. The work of Christ thrives when homes are open to God's servants. As a pastor and preacher I have been blessed repeatedly by the gracious hospitality of those who opened their homes to me.

A home can be used to draw people to Christ. When we make people feel welcome in our homes, they can more easily believe that God will welcome them into the kingdom. Telling a man God loves him is one thing. But if you invite him to break bread at a table in your home, he is much more likely to believe God loves him.

David met Larry in the gym where both men were working out. David invited Larry to his home to meet a few other men and to share in their Monday night Bible study. Touched by the welcoming spirit of the men, and hungry for a relationship with God, Larry soon gave his life to Christ.

The door to the kingdom for Larry was David's home. The genuine acceptance he received motivated him to fall in love with Jesus Christ. The home of a Christian man made a difference.

God guides people into our lives. We are not like oak leaves adrift on the sea of life. The meeting of Larry and David in that gym was not happenchance; it was a divine appointment.

The Bible tells about the Spirit guiding Paul on his missionary journeys. Forbidden to go one place, Paul had a dream. In the dream God gave him a vision of going to Macedonia to help people who were calling for him. Paul went and there in Philippi he met Lydia.

The wealthy Lydia must have had a lovely great room with a cabin on the back. The Lord opened her heart and she opened her home, saying to Paul, "Come and stay in my house." Soon she was hosting a new church in her home; the door of her home became the door to the kingdom for many new believers.

There are lonely, hurting people in every neighborhood who desperately need the hospitality of God's people. What might happen if you turned your home over to God? Imagine a group of people meeting in your home, sharing their struggles and finding rich fellowship at your table. People may meet God more easily in a loving home than at a church altar. Church furniture and stained glass windows cannot save us; God alone can save us.

If your home is dedicated to the Lord, you may meet a Larry, or a Mary, who might fall in love with Jesus through the gift of your hospitality.

The door of your home would then be the door to the kingdom for someone hungry to know God. Imagine that.

When we open our hearts to God, and open our homes for his use, amazing things can happen. Please excuse me now. Dean is calling. We must get ready for the group meeting at our house tonight. +

CHAPTER 10

Things worth doing the rest of your life

Life is about being and doing. Being has to do with our identity. Each of us must decide what it means to "be" an American or to "be" a nurse, a mechanic, a teacher, a father, a mother or a hairdresser. Being involves ideas, principles and values.

Doing is the more practical side of life. There are certain things we have to do: brush our teeth, take out the garbage, prepare and eat food or wash clothes. Then there are things that are voluntary – things you can do or not do depending on your core values.

Some things are worth doing; some things are not. Today I want to propose ten things that are worth doing the rest of your life.

1. **Encourage others.** Encouragement matters. Everybody needs it. Everybody can give it. Nobody lives well without it. People cannot survive, much less thrive, without encouragement. So look for ways to give it to somebody every day.

2. **Speak graciously to others.** Be friendly instead of rude or indifferent. Our culture is too impersonal. Resist the temptation to mimic the indifference of others. Be friendly; say "thank you." Kindness can be a breath of fresh air.

3. **Smile at people.** A frown requires more energy than a smile. Smile even when you are hurting. I smile because I don't want a stranger to say, "There goes an old sourpuss; he must have heartburn." We have a choice when we meet people. We can frown, stare indifferently or smile. So smile.

4. **Have a positive attitude.** Be positive even when others are negative. Negative talk helps no one. You will never go home at night, put your head on your pillow and say, "All that negative talk did me a lot of good today!" Positive thinking inspires others – so inspire people.

5. **Tell your friends how much they mean to you.** Your friends need to know you care. If you don't tell them, they may never know. A good friend is more precious than money. Value and cultivate friendships. We can afford to lose our possessions; we cannot afford to lose our friends. Admit it: we need each other.

6. **Do a good deed for someone in need.** A good deed can be a simple act of kindness. Call someone who is lonely. Send someone a note, a card or a letter. Share figs or cookies with someone. Take someone to lunch. Give someone who is sick or discouraged a good book or a gift card. Express your love in small and wonderful ways.

7. **Enjoy the beauty around you.** Take a moment to watch the rain fall or the tree tops swaying in the wind. Throw some cornbread to little sparrows searching for food. Admire the flowers that dare to bloom even in winter. Study the changing shapes and colors of a sunrise or a sunset. See if the moon is full. The world is filled with beauty so enjoy it!

8. **Write a few lines in your Bible.** Jot down what a certain verse or passage means to you. One day you will be gone but your Bible will still be around. Leave a few choice observations for your children or grandchildren to enjoy when they are looking through your Bible. Your faith can bless them after you are gone.

9. **Take time to pray.** Pray for your family and your friends. Pray for the people who irritate you. Pray for our nation and our leaders. Pray for understanding so that you can use your time wisely by doing things that are worth doing. Give thanks for your blessings. Enjoy what you have. Be satisfied with it. Do not envy your neighbor. Contentment is its own reward.

10. **Apply the sweet oil of forgiveness to your wounds.** Forgive yourself. Forgive people who have hurt you. Swallow your pride. Pride is an infection of the soul for which forgiveness is the best medicine. Use it liberally.

I hope you agree that these are a few things that are worth doing as long as you have breath. So, since you don't know when that last breath will be, get busy! +

CHAPTER 11

Give Up Despising Yourself

One day a long time ago God decided to populate the earth with human beings. The Bible, with beautiful imagery, explains this creation so simply that children can understand it. Almighty God, after creating order out of chaos, gathered up some dust from the ground and with his hands formed a man. Then he breathed into the man's nostrils and the man came alive.

When the work of creation was done, God looked at it and admired it. It said it was good. We are on safe ground then to conclude that a human being is a good thing and that life is a gift from our Creator. The Bible goes on to teach us that God not only likes each of us, he loves us.

Yet many people despise themselves. The truth be known, self-despising is widespread. Repeatedly I encounter people who, in agonizing despair, complain that they are worthless, having no value to anyone. Hope has vanished. Their minds are numbed by an awful sense of meaninglessness.

My heart broke to hear my father, in his declining years, ask me many times, "Why did God let me live so long?" I tried to assure him that he was alive because God's purpose for his life was not yet completed. I did my best to encourage him to trust God to the end.

Reading the Genesis accounts of creation is a great tonic for despairing souls. Here is the exciting news that the living God created human beings for a divine purpose. Human beings have value because they were created for a reason – to know God, love God and serve God.

Believing this about the origin of man generates hope. Faith grows in the fertile soil of such thinking. Embrace the teaching of Genesis about creation and you safeguard your mind against the invasion of hopelessness. Without hope, it is misery, not mercy that is fresh every morning. Without hope, nothing tastes good; nothing stirs our passion to make the most of each new day.

Settle for a lesser worldview and you are vulnerable to cynicism. The cynic buys the notion that man crawled out of a primordial swamp as a tiny amoeba and in time became an ape, finally evolving into a man. For the writer of Genesis, there is a nobler way to explain man's family tree.

If we accept the idea that our ancestors were "swamp things," then it becomes difficult to hold a lofty view of the value of human life. We become vulnerable to the belief that a human being has no more lasting significance than a stray dog on the side of the road.

If, however, our ancestors were people who talked with God, like Abraham and Moses, and Peter and Paul, then it is easier to believe that human beings were created in the image of God for a special purpose, to fulfill a plan conceived in the heart of a loving Creator.

Does Genesis offer two accounts of creation? Yes. Are these accounts conflicting? No. They complement each other, describing the creation story from two different angles. In both accounts

God is the Creator and the creation of man is the peak of God's creative work. Human beings are made in God's image, thus demonstrating the value of human life.

Genesis begins with the assumption that God exists: "In the beginning God"! Secularists insist that God is man's idea. Genesis declares that man is God's idea! Man's significance stems from having being made in the image of God. This makes humans uniquely different from animals.

The primary difference is that human beings can have a dynamic relationship with God. We can hear God, speak to God, love God, thank God, have communion with God and serve God. Humans are capable of obeying God or disobeying God. Horses and dogs cannot. Genesis helps us understand our uniqueness by underlining our power to make decisions, especially decisions that can affect the quality of our lives. Other "creatures" are not burdened by the need to obey God's commands.

Genesis pays tribute to man's capacity for reason by explaining that God asked man to name the animals and birds. The capacity to think can be used for good or ill. That we may choose to enhance our relationship with God is an exhilarating thought! To ignore the opportunity to develop a mature relationship with God is foolish misuse our intelligence.

What Genesis says about us should inspire us. God created us. He called us "good." He gave us work to do. He expects us to obey Him. He desires intimacy with us. We experience intimacy through loving obedience. We find significance in living life God's way. We see the ultimate proof of our value to God in his willingness to let his Son die on the cross for our sins. He loved us that much! So much that He wanted to give us new and richer "life" in His Son.

In the beginning God recognized man's loneliness so He created a woman. Herein we find the biblical foundation for the institution of marriage. The concept of marriage was God's idea, not an institution designed by man. In every age rebellious people weaken the moral fiber of society by undermining the sacred nature of marriage. But we need not fret. Culture changes; God's eternal Word is unchanging. His ways will survive the onslaught of evil.

What a high privilege – to cherish and use wisely the gift of life! Hopelessness cannot exist in the heart of one who believes he has value because God made him. Self-despising gives way to praising God. Negative thinking is overwhelmed by the soul's explosion of gratitude for the goodness of the loving God who gives us life! +

CHAPTER 12

Words Can Be Lethal Weapons

66 Sticks and Stones," an old children's rhyme, was composed with good intentions. Its purpose was to help a child ignore a taunt and refrain from physical retaliation. No doubt you remember how it goes: "Sticks and stones may break my bones but words will never hurt me."

The problem with the rhyme is that it is not true. Words can hurt us. Words can be lethal weapons. Vicious words can pierce the heart and cause unbelievable pain.

Grace Ketterman, a child psychiatrist, wrote a book on this subject, shattering the myth that verbal abuse "isn't so bad." In her book Ketterman describes the lethal power of careless words spoken at home, at work, in school or even at church. Words can kill, she says. They can wound a marriage, destroy a career or pierce the heart of a child.

Most of us can recall being "cut to pieces" by a verbal assault. Harsh words can suck the life out of you. A Jewish proverb says "Loose tongues are worse than wicked hands." Even more chilling is the observation of some wounded soul who said, "The tongue is like a sharp knife: it kills without drawing blood."

When it comes to verbal abuse, none of us is guiltless. We are all careless with words. The Bible confirms this. James reminds us that even devout believers make "many mistakes" in speaking. In his New Testament Letter, James writes bluntly about the unruly tongue. It is an uncontrollable "fire" that can corrupt the whole body. The tongue's fire has its origin in hell and is a tool of Satan. The devil uses the fire of the tongue to separate us from one another and from God. Divisiveness can lead to anger and hatred. Words from a loose tongue can destroy people, ruining reputations and relationships.

The tongue is so powerful, James says, that no human can tame or control it. The bewildering truth is that one day the tongue will praise God and the next day curse someone. So James laments, "Brothers and sisters, this ought not to be so"!

Is there a remedy for this problem? Yes, there is, James says. The answer is wisdom – God's wisdom. We can obtain it by asking God for it. Earthly wisdom is insufficient. Reading a hundred "self-help" books will not tame the tongue. Only God can give us the strength to tame the tongue.

The key to taming the tongue is to invite the Holy Spirit to take over. The Spirit can tame the tongue; we cannot. When the Spirit is given control of the mind and the heart, he guides us to know when to be silent and when to speak. He gives us the power to resist gossiping or to speak cruelly to others and the power to speak words of love and peace. God can use words of loving encouragement to heal wounded souls. Words of affirmation can restore those whose self-esteem has been crushed by hurtful words.

John Wesley tells of crossing a narrow bridge on horseback and finding his path blocked by another man on horseback, a man who had no use for Wesley. The man refused to back up or allow Wesley to pass, and said, "I shall not give way to a fool." Wesley replied, "Then I shall," and pulled his horse aside so the man could pass.

Wesley, the founder of Methodism, was often a wise steward of words. The Spirit helped him discern when to "yield to others" and when to speak the truth in love so that his words could produce what he called "a harvest of righteousness." With the Lord's help, we can do that also.

Though we may never become perfect in speaking, we can improve. We can invite the Spirit to inject our minds with God's wisdom so that our words are less hurtful and more pleasing to the Lord. We can learn the skill of planting seeds of peace with our words.

We can make it our heart's desire for our lips to speak words of blessing and not cursing. We can pray with the Psalmist, *"May the words of my mouth and the meditation of my heart be pleasing in your sight, O LORD, my Rock and my Redeemer."* +

CHAPTER 13

The Precious Gift of Memory

Memory is a precious gift. We are wise to treasure it, nurture it and use it. But we must guard against using it wrongly.

Remembering the mistakes of others has little value. Since we all err it is best to forgive and forget the blunders of others. And hope our friends will afford us the same kindness.

Dastardly deeds are not easily forgotten. The terrorist attack of 9-11 burns in our memory. Though memories fade with the passing of time, this heinous crime will be remembered as long as we live.

The God of the Bible calls upon his people to remember not the evil deeds of others but rather the kindness of God. The Passover Feast, for example, was begun in obedience to God's command that the Jewish people remember how God delivered them from bondage in Egypt.

Jewish families have obeyed that command for centuries, gathering in early spring every year to remember the kindness of

God. In early years the father of each family would bring a lamb "without blemish" to be slaughtered by the priests. The blood of the lamb was spilled upon the altar. The meat was returned to the father and cooked for the entire family to enjoy that night. Unleavened bread, cooked without yeast, was included in the Passover meal. The bread reminded them of their hasty departure from Egyptian slavery.

This celebration had been observed for centuries before Jesus came. But with his coming, in "the fullness of time," God did a new thing. Time was divided and a new era began.

Jesus understood his mission: he would become the sacrificial lamb, the perfect lamb. His life was unblemished by sin. No truer words were ever uttered by John than these: "Behold the lamb of God." When Jesus died upon the cross he was the lamb "slain from the foundation of the world," fulfilling the plan of God.

Judas betrayed him. The Jewish leaders insisted that he die. The disciples ran. The bloodthirsty crowd cried, "Crucify him!" The Romans scourged him unmercifully. They executed him upon a wooden cross without realizing that Jesus was giving his life for the sins of the world. His life, he said, was not taken from him.

Before this mighty deed of God occurred on Calvary, Jesus had arranged to eat a Passover meal with his disciples. We call it the Last Supper. There he explained what was about to happen before he would suffer.

During the meal Jesus took bread, broke it and gave thanks to God. Now many Christians bow their heads and offer a prayer before each meal. My parents taught my siblings and me to pray before meals. We still do, even in restaurants, holding hands and offering a quiet prayer to express gratitude to God. It is humbling to realize that we practice this habit because Jesus prayed that night in Jerusalem before breaking bread and sharing it with his disciples. We do it because he did it!

How natural it seems for a father or a mother to offer a prayer of thanks at the table, so that children may learn to take nothing for granted! I am so grateful for this legacy from my parents – the practice of prayer at mealtime. Tears of gratitude well up in my eyes as I remember my parents insisting that no one begin eating until a prayer of thanks was offered!

When Jesus had given thanks, he broke the bread, and giving it to his disciples, said those remarkable words, "This is my body, given for you: this do in remembrance of me." The meaning was clear. The breaking of the bread symbolized the breaking of his body on the cross. Every time I take Holy Communion, I tremble inside, realizing once again that Jesus died for me.

No wonder Charles Wesley cried in more than one of his hymns, "for me, for me, He died!" It is an overwhelming truth – He died for me, for you, for us all. He willingly endured the cruelest form of execution – flogging and death upon a cross – for me and for you. Does it not move you to thank him for this unmerited mercy?

What a price Jesus paid for our sins! Can we dare to forget what it cost God to make salvation available? Jesus expects us to remember him when we eat of the loaf and drink of the cup. He knows that when we remember what he did for us, we are motivated to offer our own lives as vessels of honor in his service.

Jesus died for you. Remember that. It will affect the way you live! +

CHAPTER 14

Stop Taking Yourself So Seriously

It is healthy to believe that you have value as a person, that you are important to several, perhaps many people. You make a difference in significant ways. Having confidence in your worth as a human being is a good thing.

It is, however, unhealthy to value yourself too highly, to suppose that you are the most important person on the block. The secret is to not take yourself too seriously which tends to make you uptight and miserable.

Now and then I run into people who talk incessantly, as though everybody is dying to hear what they have to say. These talkers seem full of themselves. And they hate silence so they fill the air with words, their words.

I listen as patiently as possible while wishing Scottie would beam me up to another planet. I resist the temptation to jump into the conversation with some good advice – relax and live a little; you are not the center of the universe. Stop taking yourself so seriously and have fun listening to someone else talk awhile.

It helps to remember that the world does not revolve around me. That does not diminish me in any way. I am still a person of worth. I am even unique; there is no one else quite like me.

That thought is worth a good laugh. My friends are surely thankful there is no one else like me. They would hate to have to put up with two of me.

A healthy sense of humor helps you to laugh at yourself when you make silly mistakes. Without such a disposition you can never enjoy other people or be fun to live with. Nobody enjoys being around straitlaced people who are unable to laugh at themselves.

The humorless life is one of misery filled with tension, friction, anxiety and restlessness. Those who live with such people are thirsty for laughter. They are always looking for an oasis – a caring, smiling person genuinely interested in other people.

Once we throw away visions of grandeur about ourselves, we can enjoy being an ordinary person who is both flawed and gifted. We don't have to be the smartest person in the universe. We can just be glad we are smarter than a rock and enjoy this brief life before time runs out.

When you do something dumb, you can laugh at yourself instead of beating yourself up. You can be thankful for the brains you do have. There is a good chance you have not worn them out yet. So you can use what you have instead of wishing you had more.

A great way to get a good laugh is to take a look in the mirror. Notice how much a smile does for your face. Instead of fretting that you are not more beautiful or handsome, just be thankful you don't look any worse. Enjoy the way you look. After all, what you see is all you've got so you might as well enjoy it.

One of my great challenges is to resist getting uptight about uptight people. I try to remember that I am not in charge of the behavior of other people; I have a full-time job trying to control my own. It is best to respond with laughter than anger when someone else makes a stupid mistake. Laughing with others can reduce the tension in the air and it is good therapy for the soul. And when it comes to laughing, we ought not be content with a giggle and a smile. It is good for the soul to throw your head back and enjoy a belly laugh now and then.

I love the story of the origin of "Rule 63." In the early days of AA (Alcoholics Anonymous), Bill and Bob met with a hundred recovering alcoholics to develop a charter for the organization. Eagerly, almost addictively, the group formulated rule after rule until they had 62 rules and regulations. Suddenly they realized what they had done. Their compulsiveness and addictiveness had run rampant. So, with good humor amid healthy laughter, they created Rule 63: "We will not take ourselves too seriously."

They scrapped the other rules and began the movement without the excess baggage of many rules. The great success of AA teaches us how helpful "Rule 63" can be in all our lives. If you are "the Boss" where you work, Rule 63 will help you become a better leader. People will enjoy you more. If, however, you constantly have to remind everyone that you are "the Boss," you are simply taking yourself too seriously.

The strings on a guitar or violin must be tightened in order to play well, but they will break if they remain tight all the time. The lesson of the strings – relax, loosen up, laugh a little and enjoy being alive.

True freedom is the great reward for not taking yourself too seriously. Hard work must be mixed with humor or it becomes drudgery. When the balance is right, life is rich and enjoyable. At the end of the day the losers are those who took themselves too seriously. The winners are those who were fun to be with. +

CHAPTER 15

Lessons Passed On to My Grandchildren

My friend Robert Parker spoke at his own funeral, an amazing experience for the crowd attending his graveside service. Parker, a 75-year-old retired veterinarian, died after being burned in an accident on his farm. He was a rock solid disciple of Jesus Christ and an Auburn man.

Months before his death Parker taped a message he wanted played at his funeral. The playing of his words brought strong men to tears. He spoke of his love for his family, calling out the names of his children and grandchildren and some friends. He shared what he thought was most important in life – to love God and others, to value friendships more than possessions, to give generously, to do right and to persevere in doing right.

A mutual friend, Linda Smith, said that Parker's words were powerful. "Men and women and grandchildren were crying as they heard their names called out."

At 84 I realize it will not be long before my own funeral. Parker's message to his family has prompted me not to record a message to be played at my funeral but to share in writing some of the valuable lessons I have learned about life. Since some of my children and grandchildren do not read newspapers, I am sending them this message by other means.

Solomon counseled young men with these words: "Listen to your father, who gave you life, and do not despise your mother when she is old" (Proverbs 23:22). Solomon wanted sons to listen to their fathers so that by living a good life they could bring joy to their fathers. He said, "The father of a righteous man has great joy; he who has a wise son delights in him" (Proverbs 23:24).

I listened to my father when I was young and when I became a man I began to formulate the lessons he had taught me by precept and example. Fathers teach best by example, without words. My daddy did that. He understood what Saint Francis of Assisi told his preachers: "Preach the gospel at all times. When necessary, use words."

I hope that my example has been worthy but I also feel compelled to offer in writing, to my family, the valuable lessons my daddy taught me. These lessons have helped me live a better life and they are worth passing on. Here they are:

One, remember at mealtime to thank God for what you eat. I learned this at Daddy's disciplined dinner table. My siblings and I were trained not to begin eating until Daddy had prayed.

When Daddy prayed he "said" this blessing: "Bless heavenly Father, this food to our use and ourselves to thy service, for Christ's sake, Amen." That is the only prayer I ever heard Daddy pray but he prayed it at every meal, at home and in restaurants. We held hands when we prayed. This mealtime habit taught me to honor God and to understand that food on the table is a sign of God's love.

Two, treat your wife with respect and never ridicule her. I do not remember my Daddy ever belittling Mama. Later as a husband I realized that ridiculing my wife was a serious mistake and that I needed to treat her respectfully at all times. Respect is one of the ingredients of a healthy marriage.

Three, abstain from the use of alcoholic beverages. Daddy saw his own father die young, partly from the use of alcohol. He became a teetotaler and insisted that his children follow his example. A life of abstinence has been a good choice for me since I value highly the influence of my example. The use and abuse of alcohol destroys lives and families. To use it is to risk hurting others, especially the ones you love the most.

Four, honesty is the best policy. Daddy believed that a man's word should be his bond. Cheating is always self-destructive. I am a better man for having had a father who was a man of integrity.

Five, leave your children the legacy of a good name. Solomon believed a good name is better than wealth. Daddy did not leave me a lot of things. Mama gave me one of his pocket knives and one of his walking sticks. They are important to me but not as much as the good name Daddy left me. When someone says to me, "I knew your dad," there is never anything but a compliment to follow. I want to leave such a legacy for my children.

Six, a wise man will learn to be tender as well as tough. Daddy was as tough as nails but in his later years he learned the art of tenderness. After age 60 he learned to tell me he loved me. That blessed me in ways I cannot explain. What a blessing it is to remember that, once he learned how to say "I love you," he almost never ended a conversation without speaking those precious words. I like to think that Daddy learned the need for tenderness from Saint Paul who said, "Be kind to one another, tenderhearted, forgiving one another even as God, for Christ's sake, has forgiven you" (Ephesians 4:32).

Seven, by his example Daddy taught me to overcome selfishness by living your life for others. After his death I realized that Daddy had not worked hard, from sunup till sundown, so that he could acquire things for himself. He wanted to be a blessing to his family and his community. His life reflected his belief that a man should love God and try to live like Jesus taught us to live – whether on a farm or behind a pulpit.

Daddy was not a perfect man. He had his flaws as we all do. But he taught me some lessons that have enriched my life. I am glad I listened to my father. My prayer is that my children and grandchildren will take seriously the lessons I am passing on and find in the application of them immeasurable blessings. +

CHAPTER 16

In the Dread of Winter, We Long for Spring

Baby, it's cold outside! It's freezing every night. Winter is upon us! Wrap up good before you stick your nose outside. Take the dog for a walk? In weather like this, no way!

Throw another log on the fire! Logs burning in an open fireplace can calm the soul and make you smile as you remember that if winter is here, "spring is not far behind."

Harsh though winter days may be, they will pass. The daffodils will bloom. Spring will come. The bleakness of winter will surrender to the glory of springtime.

Look again at those barren trees. Look long enough to see those tiny buds on the limbs. Those lifeless trees are playing possum. Those innocent buds will soon explode and multiply into green leaves.

In the dread of winter, we long for spring. But deep down we know it will come. It always has. It always will. And our anticipation of spring is a precious gift we can celebrate – and even cultivate.

We may not be rich but if we have the gift of anticipation we are not broke. Caught in the vice of financial bondage, we can anticipate a day when the shackles will be broken! Without anticipation, that day will never come.

Relationships may be difficult. Confidences have been broken. Feelings have been hurt. Colleagues are angry. Yet hope is not dead. Broken relationships can be restored through the painful process of forgiveness. Though it is not easy to ask for forgiveness, we know that life is impossible without a forgiving spirit. So we anticipate healing and when it occurs it feels like springtime.

There are times when nothing we do seems right. Everything goes wrong at the same time. We feel out of sync with life. But we refuse to give up – on ourselves or on others. We reach down for a fresh supply of expectation and nurture what we receive. Hope cultivated will grow. Eventually there will spring forth a renewed anticipation that better days are just ahead.

The sweetness of marriage can turn bitter overnight. We can be thoughtless. Stupid comments interrupt the flow of affection. We feel imprisoned by our own foolishness. We remember when love overflowed and our bond was heavenly. We long to recover the tender affection we once enjoyed.

That's when anticipation pays off. We expect our brokenness to be healed. Common sense helps us find ways to say, "I was wrong" and "Please forgive me." Forgiveness happens. The torment of soul ends and with tears a stronger bond emerges. And when that happens it feels like springtime!

Check your supply of anticipation. If it has run low, be thankful for what you have. Nourish it. Cultivate it and be patient. Winter never lasts forever. Spring is on the way and the expectation of it will warm your heart on these cold nights. +

CHAPTER 17

Who Controls Your Life?

Evangelist Franklin Graham came to Montgomery one day in 2016, preaching in a rally outside the state capitol. Graham's "Decision America Tour" was unique. He preached at every state capitol in the nation, calling upon Americans to turn to God as the only hope for our country.

Wisely Graham did not endorse any candidates for public office. He did urge people to cast their votes for candidates who uphold biblical principles. His message was primarily to Christians, imploring them to pray for our nation and its leaders and to vote. In every century God raises up men and women who call upon people to turn to God. This was the message of the Old Testament prophets. And for centuries we have had people like Franklin Graham calling our attention to this striking promise of God: *"If my people, who are called by my name, will humble themselves and pray and seek my face and turn from their wicked ways, then I will hear from heaven, and I will forgive their sin and will heal their land"* (2 Chronicles 7:14).

James, a leader of the church born after the death and resurrection of Jesus, called upon the Christians of his day to turn to

God. He phrased it differently by saying "Draw near to God and he will draw near to you."

Today America is sorely divided and this divisiveness could destroy our nation. The church is also seriously divided over many moral and political issues that are weakening the church's influence in society.

In these days when America is at a crossroads, Christians could with profit look again at the teaching of James in his New Testament letter. The problems America is facing are not unlike the problems that plagued the early church.

James saw that internal conflict and strife were destroying the churches for which Christ had died. He upbraids the Jewish Christians for their sinful attitudes. He urges them to repent and humble themselves before the Lord. Harmony could only be restored by such a change of heart.

What was their problem? James names two major problems: greed and pride. Notice the words James uses: "cravings," "covet," and "your pleasures." Like many of us today the early Christians wanted what they wanted and they wanted it "now." That is what happens, James says, when people chase after the world's values instead of staying focused on God. We cannot be friends of the world and friends of God at the same time.

Some of us want it both ways. We want God on our own terms. We want the world and its pleasures and we want to be spiritual enough to have God at our beck and call. James says that will not work because God is a jealous God. He will not tolerate our worship of other gods. We must worship God and Him alone. No other plan of our own making is acceptable to God. While God loves us, He opposes us when we are proud but he gives us grace when we are humble.

By "the world" James means those values and attitudes that are despicable to God. The world's values are different from those of the kingdom of God. The world influences us to oppose God, to lust for power and pleasure, and to live as we please rather than obey the commandments of God. The world encourages greed and selfishness, causing us to think only of our own desires and ignore the needs of others.

James points out that when we become friends of the world, and thus enemies of God, our prayer life is shattered. When we are not right with God, we simply don't know how to pray. We ask but do not receive because we "ask wrongly." We ask for things with the wrong motive. We want to use God rather than let God use us. When we are in synch with the world, we are out of synch with God. We cannot have it both ways. We cannot serve both God and the world. When we choose the world we drop God.

Christians do not lose fellowship with God intentionally. Satan lures us off the path of righteousness. When we are tempted, we let our guard down and give the devil a foothold. One thing leads to another on a downward spiral until one day we find ourselves at odds with God. James offers sound advice for dealing with this dilemma.

His advice is to get back to God in the certain hope that if you will draw near to God, He will draw near to you. How do we get back to God? First, admit that God has not moved! We have moved – away from God. So don't blame God. Just do what James advises: Submit to God and resist the devil. We cannot surrender to God without at the same time resisting the influence of the world's evil forces.

This is not easily done. All of us want to be in control; we do not want to submit to God or anybody. In some ways every one of us is a "control freak." The last thing we want to do is give up our self-will. But do it we must, in repentance and humility, if we truly wish to get right with God. Until that becomes our singular passion, other passions of the flesh will control us.

Celebrate Recovery is a ministry that offers help for people struggling with hurts, habits and hang-ups. The program teaches that the road to recovery is grounded in eight principles based on the Beatitudes. The third step in the program asks each person to "consciously choose to commit all my life and will to Christ's care and control." Recovery results from turning the control of one's life over to Christ!

James concurs. Humble repentance and surrender are necessary to live as authentic friends of God. When we begin to mourn over our sins, God restores our joy. Humility, repentance and surrender open the door to a new and fulfilling relationship with God.

Once our relationship with God has been restored it is necessary to remain on guard. We are easily tempted to become proud. When we are tempted, the Holy Spirit warns us. His warning is a signal to get off our high horse and draw near to God again, in humility and repentance.

Is this a once in a lifetime transaction? Absolutely not! It needs to become our lifestyle – to live in constant awareness of our need to humbly submit ourselves DAILY to the living Christ! Repentance, as John Wesley taught, is a continuing necessity for believers.

As Christ followers many of us tend to drift away from God. This means there is never a morning when I do not need to pray, "Lord Jesus, please nudge me if I start drifting away from you and give me the grace to draw near to you this very moment for nothing matters more than being your friend forever!"

Such praying could be what is needed today by both America and the church. God alone can heal the divisiveness that is destroying us. +

CHAPTER 18

Be Careful About Your Assumptions

If an assumption is assuming something to be true without proof, then we are all guilty. We make assumptions daily about things we hear and see. Sometimes we are right. Often we are wrong.

We may, for example, misjudge a person based on their appearance. Many times I have done that. And it is sobering to realize you have made false assumptions about others.

I heard a woman confess that she had misjudged a pudgy little woman who joined her church. She said, "When I first saw her I quickly assumed that she would be good for a bowl of potato salad for one of our church suppers." "But," she continued, "I felt rather stupid when within a year this chubby lady became a very effective Bible teacher in our church!"

Careless judgment of others is not an uncommon sin among those of us who serve the Lord; some of us have 20/20 vision when it comes to seeing the "speck" in a brother's eye while blind to the "log" in our own eye.

I love the story of a little girl who, years ago, was locked in the dungeon of a mental institution near Boston. Only those who were hopelessly insane were consigned to that miserable dungeon. Doctors had no hope for the girl they called "Little Annie" so she was confined to a living hell in a small cage with little light. Fortunately, the story did not end in that dungeon. An elderly nurse, nearing retirement, came on the scene, an unusual person who had hope for every child. She began taking her lunch into the dark dungeon and eating outside Little Annie's cage. She thought her presence might communicate love and hope to the pitiful little girl.

Sustaining hope for Annie was not easy. Her mistreatment in the past had triggered intense anger. Frequently she attacked anyone who came into her cage. At other times she ignored those who came near her. This was Annie's initial reaction to the elderly nurse; she paid her no attention.

One day the kind nurse left some brownies outside Annie's cage. Annie ignored them while the nurse was present but the next day the brownies were gone. After that every Thursday the nurse brought brownies to Annie. Soon doctors observed a change in Annie. They moved Annie upstairs where she continued to improve. Finally, Annie, once a "hopeless case," was told that she was well and free to leave.

To everyone's surprise Annie told them she did want to leave! The kindness of the elderly nurse had inspired Annie to believe that she could help others as the loving nurse had helped her. Annie stayed and it was she who later loved and nurtured the amazing Helen Keller out of her own dungeon.

Annie understood adversity and knew it could be overcome. She had lost most of her sight by age five. By age 10 her mother had died and her father had deserted her. She and her brother Jimmie were sent to the poorhouse. Her brother died there. Later two operations on her eyes restored enough sight that Annie was able to read normal print for brief periods of time.

Helen Keller, deaf, blind and mute, described her deliverance with these words, "I was helplessly adrift when someone took my hand, someone who would not only teach me all things, but someone who would love me." That someone was Annie, known to the world as Anne Sullivan, the woman who devoted her life to helping Helen Keller become a beautiful, useful person.

Had I seen Annie in that dungeon, and witnessed her violence, I would have assumed as the doctors did that she was hopeless. And I would have been wrong.

My mistaken assumptions have taught me that everyone I meet probably has potential that is hidden from my eyes. The amazing story of Annie helps me remember that. +

CHAPTER 19

Spring Flowers Remind Me of Mama

66 In the spring a young man's fancy lightly turns to thoughts of love." That is a famous line from the poetry of Alfred Tennyson. I suppose the British Lord was right about young men. And I can testify that it is also true for old men for spring flowers stimulate thoughts of love for my Mama.

Mama loved flowers. She grew flowers. She knew flowers. Both her thumbs were green. At one time Mama had a half acre of Daylilies. She sold some but loved to give them away to family members and friends.

Working in the yard around our country home was a passion for Mama. She turned a briar patch into a flower garden. Flowers were everywhere, surrounding the humble home which Dad built with his own hands. Hanging baskets of green ferns and flowering plants were always swaying in the breeze.

Mama loved life. While Dad was out in the fields raising cattle and growing cotton and corn, Mama was busy cooking, canning or sewing – and she loved it all. But best of all she loved working in her yard. Coming home, over the years, I usually found Mama in her yard, defending her plants against the evil weeds.

She hated nut grass. Her children and grandchildren all remember how she recruited them to serve in her war against the nut grass and weeds that tried in vain to choke her flowers.

When the aging process required a hip replacement, we figured Mama would slow down but we were wrong. Though unable to kneel she sat in a chair and continued to tend her flowers.

One day she fell in the yard and could not get up. By that time Dad was deaf as a post so her calls for help went unheeded for hours. Finally one of her daughters heard her and came to her rescue. Stubbornly she refused to stop working outside.

Canning food is dangerous work. But the danger did not deter Mama. One day Mama accidentally spilled hot paraffin on her right hand and arm. Months of painful, tedious therapy followed before she could use that hand again.

Mama's injured hand kept her out of her flower beds for awhile but she refused the role of an invalid. Her several pen pals needed to hear from her so she learned to write with her left hand! We all marveled at her grit and determination.

Dad built Mama a small green house. There she guarded her tender plants during winter months. Then, to honor Mama's devotion to flowers, Dad built her a huge green house with glass walls and ceiling. He even installed a sprinkler system and a gas furnace. She was so proud of her green house. Now she could really grow flowers!

Mama advertised and sold some of her flowers by mail and to customers who came to the house. She used the name, "Carrie's Garden," though I never heard anyone call her Carrie. She was Caroline to her friends while her 12 siblings called her "Sister."

When my flowers are at their best I wish I could talk to Mama. She was a reservoir of information. Outside my study window there thrives a running rose bush, blessing me with beautiful cascading white booms. Mama could tell me if this is a floribunda rose or a grandiflora. She would know.

Mama enjoyed her amaryllis plants. The appearance of an amaryllis bloom was a joyous moment she loved to share with others.

Near my rose bush, peaking through tall grass and gently shaded by a popcorn tree, are two bright red amaryllis blooms. These lovely blooms will not last long but while they last they will remind me how much Mama loved the amaryllis.

Mama gave me a love for flowers that has enriched my life immeasurably. I wish I had expressed my gratitude to her while she was still living. Life slips by so quickly, leaving many tender feelings unexpressed, "thoughts of love" to use Tennyson's words. So I have decided that while I have breath I will let spring flowers remind me to more boldly express the tender feelings of my heart to those dearest to me. +

CHAPTER 20

Good Habits Help Us

Good habits deliver meaning and joy to our lives. Bad habits destroy us. As I look back on my life I am thankful for the people who taught me the value of maintaining good habits.

Author and evangelist E. Stanley Jones was 76 when I met him. I was 26. I was immediately impressed with his daily schedule and personal discipline. During a five-day retreat Jones insisted on going to bed by ten o'clock each night. As the time neared ten each evening Jones would quietly excuse himself and retire to his room. He claimed that his routine was one of the secrets of his good health.

"I rise every morning at 5 o'clock," he said. "After dressing I spend time in prayer." He called this quiet time his "Listening Post," an hour spent listening to God speak to him. He was intentional, he said, about listening to God rather than "telling" God his needs.

But Jones learned the value of being flexible. His travel schedule was sometimes interrupted. One night, because his plane was hours late arriving at his destination, he got to bed at 2 a.m. Determined to follow his daily discipline, he rose at 5 a.m., dressed and began "listening" to God. With a twinkle in his eye, Brother Stanley said he heard God say to him, "Go back to bed, Stanley; you need more rest." So, obediently, he went back to bed!

This incident prompted Jones to realize the importance of being fixed in a few things but flexible in most. He explained it this way: "I am fixed in Jesus but flexible in other things." I saw in this a valuable principle for living. Being flexible rather than rigid in most things helps us get the most out of life.

I have found that life works better when I follow the same daily routine. Morning is my best time so I enjoy rising early. As soon as I am awake I try to remember to give thanks to God that I am alive for life is a precious gift.

After indulging my desire for coffee I turn to my own version of the "Listening Post." I see the morning as a time to ask for my marching orders. What does the Lord want me to do? Where does he want me to go? Who are the persons he wants me to care about today? I look to the Bible for answers to the question: What are you teaching me today? I want to become fully aware of his presence and open to his direction for my life.

Each morning my soul is stirred by remembering that God's mercies are "fresh every morning," I am constantly in need of God's mercy and am so thankful that his mercy is constantly available. It does my soul good to remember that God loves me in spite of my sins and his plans for me are good. This is an important truth to embrace in a world of unbelievable evil that manifests itself in violence, hatred, suffering and murder.

If you are reading this as the morning light is breaking, give thanks for the gift of a new day. Thank God for the good habits he has given you the grace to develop. Ask for grace to overcome your bad habits. Listen to God. Listen long enough for him to tell you how much he loves you and how he wants to make you a blessing to someone today.

Strengthen your good habits. They help you make the most of life. Remind yourself that because you are fixed in Jesus, you have the freedom to be flexible as you relate to others and deal with the challenges of your life.

Perhaps the best of all good habits is to spend time every day listening to the God who created you, loves you and wants to help you get the most out of this life so that you are well prepared for the next life. +

CHAPTER 21

The Influence of My Mothers

Each year Mother's Day reminds me to give thanks for the three women who have so greatly influenced my life. The first is my mother, Caroline Johnson Albritton. The second is Sarah Danford Brown, my wife's mother. The third is my wife, Dean, the mother of our five sons.

Last week my son Steve brought me a book he found in the attic of the home in which I grew up. The moth-eaten book is titled *Pinocchio* by Carlo Collodi. Inside the front cover is my name, obviously printed by my mother, with the date "1939." Assuming the book was a birthday gift, I was seven years old and soon to finish the first grade.

The book reminds me how my mother encouraged me to read. Using McGuffey Readers and a Bible full of pictures, my mother instilled in me a love of reading. Since this was before the arrival of television, books were my great source of adventure. I read voraciously the Rover Boys series and loved the book about Tarzan. He was one of my earliest heroes.

Mama pushed me to do well in school. I can remember reading by the light of a kerosene lamp, knowing that I had to finish my homework right after supper on school nights. Sometimes Mama would use an alarm clock to make sure I spent what she considered enough time studying. She was in control.

Though I got tired of being told what to do, I realized years later that her discipline helped me become a better person. I suppose most children get tired of being told what to do, when to be home, and to clean up our room one more time. We long to be sixteen and get a driver's license. We want to escape parental control, become adults, get married and do what we please.

When we are young we don't think much about dying and going to heaven. Heaven will be having our own home with no fastidious parents to boss us around. We long to be free of having someone saying, "Make up your bed, pick up your clothes, and take the garbage out!"

So at age twenty I persuaded my childhood sweetheart to get married. How foolish we were. We had hardly two hundred dollars between us. But Dean and I found an apartment for fifty dollars a month in Auburn, and set up housekeeping. We had very little but we had each other and I was free at last of my mother's domination.

Then I began to discover what marriage is all about. There was still a woman in the house who expected me to make up my bed, pick up my dirty clothes and take out the garbage. There was still a woman who wanted to know where I had been, where I was going and what time I would be home. There was still a woman with me who wanted me to dress neatly, behave myself and do my best.

Slowly it dawned on me that a man does not do well without a woman in his life. From infancy it had been my mother who helped me. From now on the helper would be my wife. She took over where my mother left off. My job was to figure out how to be her helper too, without sounding like her mother. Like me she needed someone to take the place of her mother in her life.

Tension took its toll during the early years of our marriage. We struggled to learn our roles in this strange thing called matrimony. I had to understand what she meant when she said heatedly, "I am your wife, not your mother!" Likewise, she had to learn what I meant when I told her in no uncertain terms, "I am your husband, not your father!" Gradually we learned the hard way how to live together.

Adjustments are seldom easy. I never dreamed that within a few years I would be living with two women. Dean's mother came to live with us and except for the time she stayed with Dean's sister Dot, she was with us until she passed away at age 99.

After the passing of our mothers I realized that God had blessed me with two mothers. Sarah was a good woman who helped me more than twice as many years as my own mother. She was not a career woman, though she did work for some years as a prison matron. Her life was her children and her grandchildren. Her greatest joy was doing something to help her family.

Sarah hated dirt. A thousand times I watched her go on a rampage against a dirty floor or a dirty refrigerator, and she always won. Our lives were better because of the tireless labor of the woman who earned the title I gave her – "Mrs. Clean."

There were many times when we did not get along well. I thought it was her fault. She was simply impossible to live with. Years later I realized that I was more difficult to live with than she was. After many wars and rumors of wars we found a way to live together. That only happened after I recognized that it was contending with me that made Sarah cantankerous at times. At long last I realized how indebted I was to her for allowing me to marry her daughter and for helping us to raise our children.

Slow learner that I am, I did finally realize how blessed I had been. I had the good fortune of having two mothers to whom I am indebted beyond my capacity to repay. One helped me for 18 years to grow up and become a responsible husband and father. The other helped me for 50 years to raise a family and pursue my calling as a pastor. I shall never forget the gracious compliment Sarah paid me one Sunday after church. She said, "Walter, you were born to preach!" It blesses me still to remember those kind words!

Caroline and Sarah played a powerful role in my life. My greatest regret is that I did not fully express my gratitude to them while they were living. I wish I had given them the joy of hearing from my own lips how much they meant to me. They both loved me beyond my deserving.

Dean, of course, is the gracious lady who has meant the most to me. While we have been married for nearly 65 years, I have known her for 79 years – since we sat near each other on the front row in the first grade.

Though words cannot adequately convey my affection for her, I often tell her how much I love her for her kindness, her faith, her patience, her unwavering love and her constant encouragement. Without her by my side I would have gone down the drain a long time ago. In tough times she has always been a pillar of strength. But she is tender as well as tough. I love it when she sits at her piano and plays old songs, for my ears, about "needing some kissing"!

So with a grateful heart I praise God for the three mothers who made me a blessed man. Thanks be to God for Dean, Caroline and Sarah! +

CHAPTER 22

Homecoming in a Country Church

Homecomings are for old-timers. Young folks could care less; they just go along for the ride. Yet an annual Homecoming Sunday still means a lot to the older generation.

Old folks enjoy seeing old friends and laughing about the changes the years have brought on. But young and old enjoy the food, a gracious spread of mostly delicious covered dishes, everything from black-eyed peas to banana pudding.

I don't remember my home church growing up ever having a homecoming Sunday. But the country churches I served as a young pastor introduced me to the importance of this special day. The plan included inviting an old former pastor back to preach. He would spin yarns about the good old days and exchange war stories with the old codgers. Kids stared at him, asking their parents who the old guy was.

Kinfolks who had moved away drove back to the old home church for homecoming. They reminisced about how things used to be and remembered friends who had died. Often there was a cemetery near the church where people strolled around reading grave stones.

After church people gathered outside under big oak trees where several long tables were laden with food. You fought flies with one hand while eating with the other. A gentle breeze brought praise for the Lord's kindness. Everybody ate too much but nobody was ashamed of it. And there was enough food left over "to feed an army." Caring women fixed plates of food to share with homebound persons or the sick.

After lunch we returned to the sanctuary to enjoy some gospel music. A quartet would shake the rafters with some foot-tapping singing while Mama banged away on the old piano. Soon everybody was smiling, singing and sweating – all the while stirring the air with a funeral parlor fan since there was no air-conditioning.

The gain may have been modest but those old-fashioned homecomings did make a difference. With the church full of people, folks took pride in the progress they had made – perhaps a new air-conditioned fellowship hall or a newly renovated sanctuary. These days we don't fight flies under oak trees. We eat just as much but we do it in air-conditioned comfort.

On the first Sunday in June Dean and I are going to an old-fashioned homecoming at the country church where it all started for us in 1953 – Neal's Chapel United Methodist Church. I am eager to find out how this small congregation is doing – and wondering what changes have occurred in 63 years.

We moved into the parsonage of the LaPlace Circuit on September 5 and I preached my first two sermons at Neal's Chapel the next day, two because they had both morning and evening services back then. In addition to Neal's Chapel, the circuit included four other churches – Bradford's Chapel, LaPlace Church in Shorter, Union and Mt. Meigs. Except for Mt. Meigs, near Montgomery, the churches were all located in Macon County. Our mailing address was Route 1, Milstead, Alabama.

We began our ministry in September rather than June because the pastor of the circuit suddenly resigned in August and moved away, without I was told even saying goodbye. I was a junior at Auburn University at the time and given this awesome responsibility by the presiding elder, Dr. W. F. Calhoun. I knew absolutely nothing about being a pastor, nor did I know how to write a sermon, conduct a worship service, a funeral or a wedding. That did not deter the good Doctor Calhoun. I guess he figured I could learn on the job as most student pastors did in those days.

I began printing bulletins on a mimeograph machine on Sunday, October 25, which was my Sunday to preach in Bradford's Chapel. My sermon that morning was titled "All the Way In." It was probably a sermon I had "borrowed" from Clovis Chappell.

To this day I remain overwhelmed by the kindness and patience of the people in those churches who put up with a poor student pastor who had so little to offer them. So on June 5 I will be thankful once again to express my gratitude for the dear saints whose love and encouragement motivated me to learn at least a little about the role of a pastor. +

CHAPTER 23

Want to Serve God? Then Arm for Battle

This ancient saying embodies an eternal truth: "My son, if you would serve God, prepare your soul for temptation." So true! All who serve God are tempted to take the easy road instead of the "straight and narrow" way.

Peter took the easy road when he followed Jesus "at a distance" during the Lord's mock trial. No doubt Peter's cowardice was born out of fear for his own life.

Peter was well aware of the bitter conflict between Jesus and the religious establishment. He had to know trouble was brewing because Jesus steadfastly refused to compromise the truth with the scribes and Pharisees. Jesus was focused. His one desire was to do the will of the Father. He aimed to please God not men.

What incredible loneliness Jesus must have endured when his disciples abandoned him out of fear that they too might be crucified. He had invested three years teaching the twelve only to have them flee, cowering in the darkness like cowards. What pain must have stabbed his soul; his beloved disciples had deserted him. Now, alone, he must walk on to do the Father's will. The mournful spiritual recognized the Lord's painful loneliness:

> *Jesus walked this lonesome valley.*
> *He had to walk it by Himself;*
> *O, nobody else could walk it for Him,*
> *He had to walk it by Himself.*

But Jesus was not the only lonely man that terrible night. Though Peter was "sitting with the guards," he was alone also, alone with the dreadful guilt of his spineless denial of Jesus. His own words ricochet in his brain like hammers pounding a gong: "Even though I must die with you, I will not deny you." Surely in shameful silence he despised himself.

All of us can identify with Peter. We have sat by the fire in that courtyard more than once. We know what it's like to give in to fear and take the easy road. We had a chance to stand up for Jesus but we remained glued to our seat. The intimidation of colleagues at work was too great so like Peter we followed Jesus "at a distance." Then, when guilt settled in, we experienced that agonizing loneliness. Alone, we gaze into a mirror and see a coward staring back.

The spiritual reminds us that like Jesus we must walk the lonesome valley alone:

> *We must walk this lonesome valley,*
> *We have to walk it by ourselves;*
> *O, nobody else can walk it for us,*
> *We have to walk it by ourselves.*
> *You must go and stand your trial,*
> *You have to stand it by yourself,*
> *O, nobody else can stand it for you,*
> *You have to stand it by yourself.*

Peter had an advantage over us – and we have one over him. He had the advantage of looking into the eyes of Jesus in that courtyard and seeing the Master offering him forgiveness and a fresh start. The look that Jesus gave Peter that night saved his life. A few years later Peter was willing to die for his faith in Jesus. He rose from the ashes of cowardice and became a fearless preacher whose courage is envied by every pastor.

Our advantage over Peter is this: we do not have to walk our lonesome valleys "by ourselves." Followers of Jesus can enjoy the strengthening presence of Jesus every step of the way. Even though no other disciple may walk with us in our trials, we have our Lord's precious promise: "Remain in me and I will remain in you." And count on this: Jesus keeps his promises!

When Karol Wojtyla served as a priest in Nowa Huta, the Communists ruled Poland. Wanting to build a church, Wojtyla planted a makeshift cross on the property. The Communist rulers angrily tore it down. At night the young priest planted another cross. It was removed. Undaunted, the young priest planted another cross, and another, and every day his people gathered there to sing and celebrate Holy Communion.

Eventually the people prevailed; the church was built and the power of communism was overthrown in Poland. The priest who would become Pope John Paul II had the courage to risk his life rather than compromise his convictions!

That may be why we admired him so: he found the courage to risk his life rather than yield to the temptation to take the easy road. While we are all tempted to follow Jesus at a distance, we can, like the Pope, refuse to yield. We can find in the strengthening presence of Jesus the courage to stand our ground rather than cut and run. +

CHAPTER 24

The Glory of Jesus

The culture of America is much like that of the first century. It does not welcome testimony about Jesus Christ. In fact such testimony is resisted to the extent that most Christians remain silent about their love for Jesus, speaking of him only in "comfortable" settings.

This was not the case in the first century when the church was born. Early Christians spoke boldly about Jesus and were willing to suffer, even to die, for the honor of speaking his name in public. So today we ask ourselves the question: How can we find the courage to boldly tell others what Jesus means to us, and what he can mean to others who will trust him?

Like many others my wife Dean has struggled with this question. In a study of chapter one of the Book of Hebrews, Dean expressed some of her insights in both prose and poetry. Her observations may be helpful as you ponder how to share with our post-Christian world "the Glory" of Jesus: "My mother took me to church when I was an infant so I have been in the Church for 84 years, but I have not been 'in Christ' for that long. We can come to church without coming to Christ. We can even sing, 'The

Church's one Foundation is Jesus Christ her Lord; she is His new creation by water and the Word,' without having a clue what that means.

"When we 'join' the Church we are asked some questions. 'Do you confess Jesus Christ as your Savior?' (Hebrews 4:14 reads 'Let us hold fast to our confession.') (The Living Bible reads 'never stop trusting Him.') 'Do you put your whole trust in His grace?' We promise to serve Him as Lord and live as faithful members of the church. Church membership, however, is but the beginning of our search to understand the glory of God that we never discover until we fall in love with Jesus.

"Here is my poetic attempt to describe the glory of God that I found by falling in love with Jesus:

> Pictures cannot describe or frames fully hold
> Your marvelous love for us to see.
> How can mere books your story unfold
> Or how can I tell what you mean to me.
> My words fail to express
> The thing I know you to be,
> My stammering tongue must confess
> That I am overwhelmed by your love for me.
> When I think of new life you give
> To those who heed your call,
> My greatest wish is so to live
> That I give you my life, my all.
> My heart aches when I look around
> To those who never speak your name.
> I pray for a language profound
> So I can tell other why you came.
> Oft when day is o'er and work is done
> I wish for your face to behold,
> Then I would know if the victory's won
> When your story I have told.

"Explore with me what the gifted writer of Hebrews says in chapter one. He reminds us that while God 'spoke' his plan for his people through the prophets, he has now spoken to us through his Son. What follows are some of the most profound words about Jesus ever penned:

1. **God has appointed Jesus Christ <u>His heir</u>.** He is Heir to all things. He is the firstborn heir of God. Paul says that we are joint heirs with Christ and if we suffer with Him so then we also will be glorified with Him. That means Christ shares his glory with us.

2. **Through Jesus Christ God <u>made the universe</u>.** He created all things. Before anything else existed, Christ was with God, sharing in the creation of the world.

3. **The Son is the radiance of <u>God's Glory</u>.** God's Glory is like a great beacon light   The Son is the radiance, the rays of light, that shine out from that beacon. Let me try to express this 'revealing light' in poetic terms:

As the rays of sunlight
Come shining into a darkened room,
So God's light frees the soul from night
That we may not walk in gloom.
The glimmering light spills
Over our innermost parts
To show us what God wills
For our sinful hearts.
The rays search out every shadow
That lingers still to lure,
But God is ready to bestow
His love to make us pure.
Slowly the sins that we concealed
Are laid at the throne of Grace.
There the Holy Light revealed
The radiance of His face.

4. **Jesus Christ is the <u>exact representation</u> of God's being.**
    The Son himself is God. The Son is the perfect picture of
    God. When we want to know what God is like, we look
    at Jesus Christ. Jesus himself said, 'He who has seen me has
    seen the Father.'

5. **Jesus Christ <u>sustains all things</u> by His powerful word.**
    It is He who holds everything together. When we study the
    atom we find that there is a force that holds it together. Jesus
    is this 'force' and much more. He holds me together! He is
    the great 'glue' of the universe! During many 'long nights' in
    my life Jesus has held me 'together, helping me deal with sin
    and death. Here is how I have tried to express my gratitude
    poetically in a piece I titled 'Long Night':

    As I crouch with covers
    O'er my head,
    I ponder my fears and
    The things I dread.
    In my tomb of darkness, no light
    Filtering in,
    I come to grips with death and sin.
    Things look so grim in the middle
    Of the night.
    You wonder if the sun will ever
    Shed its light.
    So the soft breathing of my child
    Comes into my coverlet cave.
    What devil caused these covers piled
    As if they alone could save?
    Where is the strength for which
    I long?
    There are those who need me strong,
    Not hovering like a coward

And weak.
Where is the faith for which
I seek?
With Christ within I need
Not fear,
New strength I gain with Him
So near.
He is with me in
The night.
He covers me with His Light.

6. **Jesus Christ <u>saves us from our sins</u>.** Through His redeeming death on the cross Jesus paid the price for our salvation. I took Jesus as my Savior. He is the One who provided a way out of my sins. The Son's purification for sins includes both forgiveness for past sins and a heart-cleansing that empowers Christians to live a life of holiness. Jesus willingly gave himself to God to die for our sins – The perfect sacrifice!

7. **Jesus Christ <u>sat down at the right hand of the Majesty</u> in heaven.** Having sat down He indicated that the work of redemption is complete and He is ruling with God, the Father, over all. His enemies are being made a footstool for His feet. He is our perfect sacrifice, our perfect Savior, our perfect Priest. He has gone into heaven and is at the right hand of God, with angels, authorities and powers made subject to Him. What a Savior!

"There is a power that is beyond our imagination, so great, so wise, so wonderful, yet so close, finger-tip close to us, that we can reach out and take hold of it by faith. We can receive it and become brand new. His divine power gives us everything needed for life and godliness. He calls us by His own Glory to live glorious lives – and to explain as best we can his Glory to those who are still living in darkness! Let us find ways to do it so that others can with us be blessed by the radiance of His face!" +

CHAPTER 25

Lessons My Daddy
Taught Me

Father's Day reminds me of my indebtedness to my daddy. He taught me some valuable lessons about life.

Dad was born May 7, 1901, in Fort Mead, Florida. His parents named him Walter Matthew Albritton. His education came from the School of Hard Knocks. His first job was in a phosphate mine near his birthplace. Later he worked as a plumber's helper and picked up some carpentry skills.

Soon after marrying my Mama, Caroline Johnson, Dad moved to Alabama and began farming. He learned to farm by trial and error during the Great Depression. The skills he acquired in farming led eventually to his being hired to manage the Elmore County Farmers Exchange in Wetumpka.

I never called Dad "father." To his children he was Daddy and when we were growing up Daddy was our Rock. He was always there. The farm was his life. He worked from daylight till dark. He and Mama grew most of the food we ate and canned vegetables with a passion.

Daddy had strong moral convictions. Having seen his own father die of alcoholism, Daddy was a teetotaler all his life. He was strictly opposed to drinking, smoking, chewing tobacco and cursing. Mama shared his convictions and those beliefs became rules for our family.

Daddy died of "old age" January 24, 1995. He was 93. He and Mama had been married almost 68 years. They took their marriage vows seriously. None of us can remember them speak of divorce. Marriage was a sacred bond, a covenant with each other and God.

Though Daddy lived 93 years I still miss him. I wish I could talk to him one more time. There were conversations we never finished. But life is like that – one relinquishment after another from the cradle to the grave. One by one we must say goodbye to the family and friends we have loved until it is our turn to embrace death.

On this Father's Day I am thankful for the love and respect of my children and their mother. Simple Father's Day gifts are nothing compared to words spoken with love. The scent of Aqua Velva is soon gone. An expression of love remains in the heart. Daddy left no inheritance for us to squabble about. He simply left everything to Mama. I wish he had left me a watch or a pocket knife or a walking stick, but he did not. He left such decisions to Mama.

Mama gave me one of Daddy's old walking sticks and I cherish it. She said it was the "last one." I don't need "stuff" to help me remember Daddy. His wisdom is stored in my memory bank. Though he had little formal education, he was one of the wisest men I have ever known. So I will carry his sage advice with me to the grave. Many of his words are etched indelibly in my mind. Here are a few of Daddy's lessons that impacted my life:

1. **"Money is not the secret to a happy life."** Daddy grew up poor and raised his five children during the depression. He was not miserly but he taught us not to expect something for nothing. Only those who work hard will ever have any money; it is the fruit of labor. He believed that. His strong work ethic inspired us all. Daddy taught us the value of a dollar.

2. **"If you can't do it right, then don't do it at all."** Daddy was never satisfied with shoddy work. There was a right way to do everything and he insisted on doing any task the right way. Do your best – always. Never settle for anything less. If it means tearing something down and starting over, then do it.

3. **"Always check the oil before you start an engine."** To this day I cannot crank up a piece of machinery - whether a tractor or a chain saw - without checking the oil level. Take good care of what you have, he insisted.

4. **"Alcohol makes a man a fool."** Daddy drank tons of coffee. That was his favorite drink, with "just a little cream, not too much." He never used sugar in his coffee. His dad's alcoholism inspired his rule to have no alcoholic beverages in our home. Having seen so many lives ruined by alcoholic beverages, I am thankful for the way I was raised. Daddy was not a diplomat nor did he believe children had a vote about house rules. He laid down the law: "As long as you put your feet under my table, you will abide by my rules." His word was law. Was he wrong? You decide. All of his five children have practiced total abstinence.

5. **"Never talk back to your mother."** In his presence none of his children ever "sassed" Mama. If we did, Daddy did not spare the rod. We grew up understanding that Mama deserved our respect.

6. **"Hard work never killed anybody."** Daddy worked from sunup 'til sundown. He had no tolerance for laziness. He worked hard all his life and he expected the same from everyone else. No exceptions. In his late eighties he worked a two-acre garden and wished it was bigger.

7. **"A man's word is his bond."** Dad valued honesty. Keep your word. If you tell someone you will do something, then do it or die trying. Dad had no respect for a liar.

8. **"Always put tools back where they belong; they have a way of walking off if you leave them lying around."** A job was never finished until tools had been cleaned and returned to the place where they belonged.

9. **"Pick up that string; you may need it."** Notice a nail, a screw, or a piece of string – then pick it up and save it. Even the least little thing may have value later on. Daddy never felt comfortable with our "throw away" society.

10. **"You need a college education."** Daddy worked hard for a reason. Not for a "place on the lake." He wanted his children to have a college education, something he never had. As I grew up there was never any doubt about my going to college. He promised to help us financially - as long as we remained single. "Once you get married, you are on your own." I got married when I was a sophomore at Auburn, and he kept his word.

Daddy was impatient and hard as nails at times. But we knew he loved us and we loved him. His good qualities outweighed his weaknesses. A list of them I will not compile in the hope that my sons will do me the same favor.

Daddy was not liberal with compliments but he did give them occasionally. So I remember with joy those times when he blessed me by saying, "I'm proud of you, son." Sage advice sprinkled with a little praise. Not a bad legacy. Not bad at all. And a walking cane to boot.

A final word: if your dad is still alive, tell him you love him, while you can. That will mean much more than a bottle of Aqua Velva. +

CHAPTER 26

God Bless America!

Every Sunday my church family sings "God Bless America!" Every Sunday? Yes, every Sunday. Like it or not, it has become ritual for my congregation.

I view it as a prayer in song, a prayer of gratitude for the many ways God has blessed our land. And it is a prayer of petition, people asking God to continue blessing America.

As we celebrate the 4th of July we should move beyond celebration to gratitude, giving thanks to God for the favor he has shown our nation. Fireworks are fine although it grieves me that on this one day of the year we will spend over 600 million dollars on fireworks. In light of our national debt that seems ridiculous.

When our children were small we usually bought some fireworks. It seemed the thing to do. Everybody was doing it. But I have not bought any fireworks for many years. It is enough, and safer, to watch the dazzling displays on television.

Like many other Americans our family will gather for a cookout on the 4th and enjoy hot dogs, ribs, watermelon, iced cream and ice tea. We will groan about the heat and the flies and thank God if we get a little rain.

The celebration of this national holiday gives us a break from the heat of summer and a chance to thank God that the great American "experiment" is still working.

Though secularists continue to rewrite American history, it remains true that our ancestors came to America to find religious freedom and to establish a Christian nation. They invoked the help of almighty God to build a nation founded on biblical principles.

While there continues to be much public debate about the Ten Commandments, there is no doubt that our founding fathers considered the Ten Commandments the essential foundation stones of American government.

President James Madison, who was called the "Father of Our Constitution," said, "We have staked the whole of all our political institutions upon the capacity of mankind for self-government, upon the capacity of each and all of us to govern ourselves, to control ourselves, to sustain ourselves according to the Ten Commandments of God."

I am convinced that the more we surrender our reverence for the Ten Commandments, the more the moral fabric of our nation will unravel.

Ignorance is a dangerous thing. Some, for example, believe that "separation of church and state" is part of our constitution, but the phrase does not appear anywhere in the constitution. The brave men who signed the Declaration of Independence did not wish for America to be separated from God. They believed that America could not survive without the aid of almighty God. Historic records affirm that they believed this. Wisely our founding fathers insisted that "the state" should not be under the rule of "the church."

Despite our moral slide toward decadence, there is much about America for which we can be thankful. Every time we handle money we are confronted with our motto, "In God We Trust." This motto reminds us that our trust must not be in the power of the state but in the power of almighty God.

Religious holidays are recognized nationally. Good Friday and Christmas are actually Christian holy days. Though they are grossly commercialized, they are still woven into our culture, reminding us of the birth of our Savior and his crucifixion for our sins.

Thanksgiving remains a national holiday. From the beginning our presidents have called upon our people to give thanks to God for our blessings on this November Thursday.

Chaplains continue to be appointed to serve in Congress and in the Armed Forces. In June of 2016, the Senate Chaplain, the Rev. Patrick J. Conroy, included this petition in his opening prayer in the Senate Chamber: "As all Americans prepare to celebrate the Fourth of July, may we be forever grateful for the benefits we share as citizens of a common Nation with uncommon diversity. Help us to work together to build a better community as a light for the world." And may we all say, Amen!

I am proud to be a citizen of a nation in which godly men of the cloth have the honor of offering spiritual guidance to our senators and other congress members. Thankfully our nation recognizes that our military forces need spiritual guidance. Some of the finest men I have known have served as military chaplains.

The phrase, "one nation under God," remains in our Pledge of Allegiance to the flag even though some folks want it removed. I feel a surge of pride every time I salute the flag. Too many people have died defending the flag for me to gaze upon it with anything but reverence. Those who burn the flag disgrace themselves and deserve to be punished for such sacrilege.

While secularists wish to secularize America by removing all references to God, I do not believe they will succeed because most

Americans are not willing to renounce their godly heritage. Most of us want to live in a nation that is "under God."

We may then on the Fourth of July invoke the blessing of almighty God on what William Penn called "An Holy Experiment in Government." This experiment remains a noble enterprise that deserves our support and our prayers. We can enjoy the fireworks and watermelons but unite in praying earnestly, God bless America! +

CHAPTER 27

Does God Care When We Grieve?

The grief that follows the death of a loved one is a universal human experience. Sorrow is the twin sister of death who shatters our joy with sadness and tears. Faith is tested. Bewildered and broken, grieving souls wonder if there is a God who cares when we grieve. Bitterness can take over.

Consider the biblical story of Naomi. Like the other people in the Bible, Naomi had no last name. She was simply Naomi. When Naomi's husband Elimelech dies, she is left a widow to raise two sons alone. Ten years later both her sons are dead. All she has left are two daughters-in-law, Orpah and Ruth.

Hearing that things are better back home, Naomi decides to return to the land of her birth. She had left in a time of famine. Now bread is scarce where she lives. So, bitter and resentful, Naomi turns her despairing heart toward home.

The scene is heartbreaking. Assuming she may never see them again, she bids a sad farewell to Orpah and Ruth. All three women embrace, weeping aloud. Then the unexpected happens. An emotional Ruth insists on going with Naomi. She will not let go of her mother-in-law.

Her speech has become a classic, her words recited or sung at countless weddings despite the fact that Ruth was not talking about marriage. It was her rationale for refusing to be separated from Naomi. Her words, while lovely, are used out of context when injected into a wedding ceremony.

The next time at a wedding you are moved by Ruth's tender cry of affection, remember that she was not addressing her husband when she said:

"Entreat me not to leave you, or to turn back from following after you; for wherever you go, I will go; and wherever you lodge, I will lodge; Your people shall be my people, and your God, my God. Where you die, I will die, and there will I be buried. The Lord do so to me, and more also, if anything but death parts you and me."

One striking thing about the Bible's little Book of Ruth is that God is seldom mentioned. Ruth evidently has no personal relationship with God but speaks of Him as Naomi's God. She does imply that she wants "your God" to become "my God," so she is open to a relationship with God.

The Book of Ruth has a surprise ending. God's Big Picture emerges. Naomi's story is more than a story of grief and loyalty. It is a part of God's Story, his plan for the salvation of the world. The large role that God is playing behind the scenes is revealed in the writer's stunning conclusion.

Ruth marries Boaz. They have a son and name him Obed. Naomi becomes Obed's nurse. And who is Obed? He is the father of Jesse, the father of David. For a while we think this is the story of Naomi and Ruth or of Boaz and Ruth. Then we discover that it is much more; it is one small chapter in the Greatest Story Ever Told – the Story of Jesus!

The book does remind us that God can help us with grief. Naomi could turn to God for help. We can do more. We can turn to God in Christ. We can turn, as believers, to the Christ who indwells us. That Naomi could not do.

Though our knowledge is finite, we know much more about God than Naomi did. We know that God is like Jesus. We are aware of the tender love of God for his sorrowing children for He made that love known through His Son as he walked among us. In the days of the prophets the Jews believed the coming Messiah would be like a shepherd, gently caring for the lambs. When Jesus came that hope became a reality. The Good Shepherd walked among us and we beheld His glory! We realized that God was in Christ, reconciling the world and revealing to the world His true nature.

The God to whom we turn is a loving Father, a concept barely known to Naomi and her kin. We have a hope, a living hope much greater than Naomi's for our hope is "built on nothing less than Jesus' blood and righteousness."

When sorrows "like sea billows roll," we are held steady by the unseen Hand of our Savior. He gives us blest assurance that "it is well with my soul." Transformed by the living Christ, we can stand "on Jordan's stormy banks" and be delivered from the bitterness of grief and the fear of death. We can sing songs that Naomi never sang, such as the great gospel melody:

When I shall reach that happy place,
I'll be forever blest,
For I shall see my Father's face,
and in his bosom rest.

Knowing the Savior makes us keenly aware of the kindness of God. That kindness invites us to walk in this life with Jesus, buoyed by the hope that when our battle is over and the race is won, we shall, in the words of Fanny Crosby, "see Him face to face and tell the story – Saved by grace"! +

CHAPTER 28

Broken Promises Can Have a Silver Lining

Trust is a precious gift. Believe I mean what I say and you bless me. But if I break my promises to you, I will lose your trust. Trust, once violated, is difficult to restore. And genuine relationships are impossible without trust.

Christian marriages are usually solemnized at a church altar. The bride and groom stand before a minister who invites them to vow to be faithful to each other. The wording of the ritual leaves no room for flippancy: "forsaking all other keep thee only unto her (or him) so long as you both shall live."

Broken marriage vows usually lead to divorce and broken hearts. "Broken" signifies pain and misery. In marriage the goal is for the "two to become one." Divorce "breaks" this oneness, leaving both husband and wife wounded.

The highway of life is littered with broken promises. Business partnerships are shattered when promises are violated. Churches are sometimes destroyed or weakened when sacred vows are not kept.

Most of us take the promises of politicians with a grain of salt. We have heard too many whose campaign promises were ignored after the election.

The pain of broken promises can prove valuable, however, if the unfaithfulness of others prompts us to seek out the unbreakable promises of God. You might call this the "silver lining" of broken promises.

Christian worship is a celebration of God's faithfulness. God is faithful. This is one of the bedrock truths of Christian faith: God keeps his promises. You can count on it.

A trusted friend may betray you. Your landlord may go back on his word. Your employer may close down his business, leaving you without a job. The stock market may fail, depriving you of investments you had planned to live on in retirement. Perhaps that is why the Psalmist says, "Some trust in chariots, and some in horses: but we will remember the name of the LORD our God" (Psalm 20:7). Ultimately we learn that we cannot trust in horses, or in men, but in God alone.

The stories of Jesus' birth remind us that God keeps his word. He kept his word to Joseph and to Mary, to Zechariah and Elizabeth and to the lowly shepherds. God surprises everyone by sending angels to announce the birth of his Son to the shepherds, common laborers with no influence and no credentials. Startled and afraid, the shepherds hurried into Bethlehem to see if they could find the infant Messiah lying in a cow's stall. There they found everything just as the angels had said. Returning home, they told others that God had done just what he said he would do. Mary and Joseph could testify to God's faithfulness. The shepherds could testify to God's faithfulness. Through the centuries the saints of God have testified to God's faithfulness.

But enough of angels, shepherds and saints. The pertinent question is this: can you testify that God keeps his promises? I can. Let me explain.

As a young man I felt burdened by my sins. I thirsted for God's forgiveness. So I decided to believe his promise to save me if I trusted him. That promise is found in Romans 10:9 - "That if you confess with your mouth, 'Jesus is Lord," and believe in your heart that God raised him from the dead, you will be saved." I did that and found peace with God.

Over the years I have often grown weary of trying hard to "be a Christian" in my own strength. But I learned to trust the promises of Jesus. I found rest by believing this promise to be true: "Come to me, all of you who are weary and carry heavy burdens, and I will give you rest" (Matthew 11:28).

When I have struggled with defeat and disappointment I found hope by turning my problems over to the Lord. I believed his promise: "But blessed are those who trust in the Lord and have made the Lord their hope and confidence. They are like trees planted along a riverbank, with roots that reach deep into the water" (Jeremiah 17:7-8).

When my heart has been broken by tragedy, I have believed that God never forsakes me and is always working for my good. I believed his promise: "And we know that God causes everything to work together for the good of those who love God and are called according to his purpose for them" (Romans 8:28).

In recent years as my physical strength has sometimes failed, I have believed his promise: "He will keep you strong right up to the end, and he will keep you free from all blame on the great day when our Lord Jesus Christ returns. God will surely do this for you, for he always does just what he says, and he is the one who invited you into this wonderful friendship with his Son, Jesus Christ our Lord" (1 Corinthians 1:6-9, New Life Translation).

There it is: all the assurance I need to believe in the faithfulness of God – "he always does just what he says"! Paul saw it and the Lord let me see it!

The world needs to hear the testimonies of believers that in a world of broken promises, God is faithful. We can trust him. He keeps his promises! +

CHAPTER 29

Seek to Be Wise, Not Happy

Some translations of the Bible can be confusing. For example, the New King James Version translated Proverbs 3:13 as follows: "Happy is the man who finds wisdom...."

The word "happy" is the problem. Recent translations translate the Hebrew word as "blessed" thus rendering Solomon's advice to be "Blessed are those who find wisdom...."

Happiness is not God's ultimate will for our lives. "Happy" is rather superficial compared, for example, to "joy," as in "the joy of the Lord."

Acquire the wisdom of God, Solomon says, and you will be blessed with fulfillment, joy and contentment. Harmony with God results from applying his wisdom to the living of our days. Restless we are until and unless we begin to live by God's directions for life.

Trust is the key. We are never really "wise" until we begin trusting God. Some of us are slow learners. We want our way, not God's way. We are stubborn, thus stubborn sinners reluctant to let God have the wheel. Wise we are when at last we say, "Lord, you take over; you drive please."

The longer we hold out to run our own lives, the more un-wise we are. We trust in ourselves and fail. We trust in others and are betrayed. We trust in wealth and find no lasting fulfillment. We trust in one cause or another and the end is disappointment.

My friend Grady Rowell is a wise man. Not perfect but wise. He closes his letters with the words found on our coins: *In God We Trust.* Grady understands that life works best when we trust God. Like Grady, then, we are wise to trust God when the way is dark, when our burdens are heavy, when our heart is broken, when our job is insecure, when our friends mistreat us, when our enemies persecute us and when death comes calling.

One of the most beloved of all proverbs is 3:5-6: *"Trust in the Lord with all your heart and lean not on your own understanding; in all your ways acknowledge him, and he will make your paths straight."*

Some poet expresses this same idea this way:

I may not know God's plan for me
Each hour of every day.
But I will leave the choice with Him,
And trust Him all the way.

Solomon insists that God is quite willing to share his wisdom with us. God waits for us to "call out for insight and cry aloud for un-derstanding." When we "search for it as for hidden treasure," we find the wisdom we need.

God's wisdom, says Solomon, will "save you from the ways of wicked men, from men whose words are perverse, who leave the straight paths to walk in dark ways, who delight in doing wrong and rejoice in the perverseness of evil, whose paths are crooked and who are devious in their ways." That needs no exegesis!

Imagine how different a young man's life will be if at an early age he takes seriously this promise of God: "My son, do not forget my teaching, but keep my commands in your heart, for they will prolong your life many years and bring you prosperity."

The man is a fool who imagines himself wise and feels no need of God. Such a man should heed the advice of Solomon:

Do not be wise in your own eyes; fear the Lord and shun evil. This will bring health to your body and nourishment to your bones. . . . My son, do not despise the Lord's discipline and do not resent his rebuke, because the Lord disciplines those he loves, as a father the son he delights in.

If we ignore the necessity, and the privilege, of acquiring God's wisdom, we will likely stumble and fall, sometimes tragically. A wise father will help his children to grasp the meaning of these profound words of Solomon:

Blessed is the man who finds wisdom, the man who gains understanding, for she is more profitable than silver and yields better returns than gold. She is more precious than rubies; nothing you desire can compare with her.

I wish I had done a better job of persuading my sons to embrace the wisdom of Solomon so that they in turn might convince my grandchildren to drink from this well of wisdom. But I do not despair for I know that if somehow I can practice God's wisdom, even in old age, then my example may be more persuasive than my pleadings. +

CHAPTER 30

Troubles We Must Not Avoid

Life confirms the truth of what Jesus said about trouble. Jesus said, "In this world you will have trouble." Most of us would agree that no truer words were ever spoken.

Trouble, of course, comes in various sizes and colors. A wise man once said there are three kinds of troubles: troubles we can avoid, troubles we cannot avoid, and troubles we must not avoid.

Troubles we must not avoid are troubles that can help us, trials from which we can learn and grow and become better people. So there are lessons that only certain troubles can teach us. Those are the trials we must not avoid.

When our troubles overwhelm us we quickly tire of having so many lessons to learn. We may look at our troubles the same way Charlie Brown did one day at the beach. Charlie Brown, that lovable character of the comic strip "Peanuts," was building a beautiful sandcastle. After working on it all day he stands back to admire his work when the castle is suddenly consumed by a huge wave.

Looking at the mound of sand that minutes before was his sandcastle, and with that familiar forlorn look on his face, Charlie Brown says, "There must be a lesson here, but I don't know what it is."

A positive attitude helps us learn the lessons the good Lord is teaching us through our troubles. Thomas Edison had the attitude we all need. Edison was 67 when he watched helplessly as his laboratory burned to the ground. Staring at the roaring fire, Edison said to his son, "Go get your mother quickly. She may never see a spectacular fire like this again."

After watching his life's work destroyed by the fire, Edison went to bed, slept well and the next morning called his staff together. He calmly said to them, "We will begin again; it will be better." Like Edison, we can refuse to allow our troubles to defeat us. We can start over.

An army general had the right attitude. Zig Ziglar tells the story of a general who found himself completely surrounded by enemy troops. Rather than surrendering or panicking, the general turned to his soldiers and said, "Men, for the first time in the history of this military campaign, we are in position to attack the enemy in all directions." A sense of humor in a tough situation is a great asset!

We will all have moments when there seems to be no way out of the troubles we face. But in those times we can call upon the Lord to do what the song says he can do: "make a way where there is no way." Often this may be the best prayer we can pray: "Lord, make a way where there is no way, and give me the courage to follow where you lead me."

An easy life is not the answer. We learn more from our failures than our success. When times are hard we learn what really matters. Testing strengthens us and produces character.

I love a story that illustrates the attitude we need in order to learn and grow from life's tribulations. The story begins with the British missionary Robert Moffatt who long ago explored Africa and became passionate about sharing the Gospel of Christ with that continent. Returning to England Moffatt said "I have stood on a mountain top in Africa and have seen the smoke of a thousand villages where no white man has ever been."

A young man named David Livingstone heard Moffatt utter those words and was motivated to answer the call. Livingstone went to Africa and plunged more deeply into the African jungles than anyone before him had ever dared. But an easy life it was not; lesser men would have given up, refusing to endure the missionary's daily struggle to survive.

During Livingstone's years in Africa some folks back in England offered to send others to help him, if "there is a good road to get to where you are." Livingstone's reply became famous: "If the people you propose to send must have a good road to get here, then I cannot use them." People who require an easy road are poor students in the school of hard knocks.

When my flesh pleads for a trouble-free life, I need to remember that an easy life is not a good teacher. If I face trouble with the right attitude, and humbly ask the Lord to help me, I can become a better person while confronting the troubles I must not avoid. +

CHAPTER 31

Mentors Help Us Believe in Ourselves

A mentor is a wise and trusted teacher or counselor. The key word is "trusted." Mentoring occurs when a student admires and believes in a counselor's instruction.

Mentors give us self-confidence. An example of a great mentor is Bela Karolyi, legendary coach of the US Women's gymnastics team. In Olympic competition, as his gymnasts step up to perform, you can hear Karolyi quietly saying, "You can do it! You can do it!"

Those four powerful words can motivate people to do their best in almost any endeavor. To have someone believe in you does for your mind what eating spinach did for Popeye's body. To a large extent success requires confidence in your own ability to achieve your goals.

I learned the basic lessons of life from my parents. They taught me to value family, farm life, good food, reading, honesty, worship, relationships and hard work. In my adulthood I realized that without ever using the words, my parents had mentored me to believe in myself. They never belittled me or criticized me to the extent that I doubted my self-worth.

When I was 13 I met "Brother Si" Mathison. He was my pastor, the first preacher who took an interest in me. He was more than the man who preached on Sundays. He "connected" with me. For the first time in my life I became interested in my spiritual life Though I did not recognize it at the time, Brother Si became my spiritual mentor. I admired him but even more I trusted him; he knew my name and I could talk to him. In time he became the most important influence in my life – the role model who sparked a desire in me to become a pastor. I never lost the desire to be like him.

During his last years Brother Si spent some time living at Wesley Gardens Retirement Home in Montgomery. I visited him there more than once. We talked and prayed together. I thanked him for his friendship and his prayers. He had prayed for me daily for half a century. His wife Mary and his sons John Ed and George had been like family to me since my teen years.

When Brother Si died I was unable to attend his funeral. My disappointment was tempered by my conviction that Brother Si would not be there either. He was already in the company of the Father. His sons, like brothers to me, would merely celebrate his life and bury the body of the man who had been my spiritual father. For 50 years Brother Si had been to me what Saint Paul had been to Timothy, a wise and trusted counselor, teacher, friend – and mentor of the first order.

Brother Si taught me, as the Apostle Paul taught Timothy, to trust the counsel of the Bible. That was important since our culture, much like Timothy's culture of the first century, is prone to question the authority of the Bible. A preacher who doubts that God inspired the scriptures is like a lost ball in high weeds.

Brother Si motivated me to believe that the Bible is the inspired Word of God. From that conviction I have never wavered.

Mentoring can be expanded to include persons we know only through their writings. Elton Trueblood, the Quaker philosopher, persuaded me to think of deceased persons like Martin Luther, John Wesley, Thomas a Kempis, Oswald Chambers and others as mentors.

This idea allows me to embrace Saint Paul as not only Timothy's mentor but my own as well. As I read his wise counsel in the Bible, Paul becomes another mentor and role model for living my faith.

Look back over your life and name your mentors and role models. Give thanks for those who said, in many different ways, "You can do it!" And consider yourself especially blessed if you live long enough to hear some younger person say, "Thank you for mentoring me." +

CHAPTER 32

Got Time to Hear a Good Story?

I love a good story. I love to tell a good story. My best sermons include good stories. My "almost really good" sermons, my wife tells me, are the ones that "needed a good story."

Old people repeat stories. Younger people laugh at them for doing that. When I get old I hope my family will gently remind me not to tell the same story over and over.

There are, however, good stories that are worth repeating. So I reckon the secret is to tell such stories no more than once a year. That is my goal. I don't want to lose my best stories; in every audience there are a few dear souls who have not heard my treasured stories.

Truly good stories touch the heart. They stir the soul. And they remind us of our own breathtaking, and heartbreaking, real life experiences. A good story prompts us to think, "Yes, I know how that feels."

Recalling beautiful moments can often rescue us from despair and help us face the latest heartache with courage. When misery hovers near it helps to remember that "this too shall pass." A little fortitude, mixed with the grace of God, can help us find a way through the dark cloud of the moment. Flying has taught me that there is often brilliant sunshine just above the darkest cloud.

Beautiful moments often occur during painful experiences. If we cherish them and store them in our hearts, they can help us when trouble comes, as it surely will. So at the risk of sharing stories you may have already heard me tell, allow me to share two beautiful moments in my life.

Some years ago my wife was critically ill in a Pensacola hospital. I was deeply troubled. Her doctor was worried and not sure what to do next. The needs of our four small boys kept me from being where I wanted to be, by her side. A week after being hospitalized, Dean was still very sick.

On the eighth day things changed. As I walked into her hospital room she greeted me with a beautiful smile and said quietly, "I am well. The doctor said I can go home today." I was stunned. The day before she was so sick her life seemed to hang in the balance. How could this be?

She took my hand and explained. "Yesterday afternoon I felt terrible. It was hot and stuffy in the room. My nurse opened the window and soon I felt a gentle breeze. Suddenly I felt a Presence in the room and in my mind I heard a voice say, 'you are well, my child.' Then I realized I felt well. I did not feel sick anymore. I knew I was well." And she was!

Explain that any way you wish. I have never tried to analyze it; I just said "Thank you, Lord." That is enough for me.

Remembering that moment energizes my faith when hard times come around again. If it happened once, through no merit of my own, it could happen again. And frankly I have not been shy about asking the Lord to do it again. He is able, you know. This is his world and he is in charge.

The other beautiful moment happened almost 50 years ago but it is still fresh in my mind. About three o'clock one afternoon I told my wife and our sons I would be back before midnight. I had a speaking engagement in a town about a hundred miles away. As I started out the door our youngest son, Steve, asked if he could go with me. "Sure, son," I said, "Come on."

As we made our way down the highway I turned the car radio on. Steve reached up and turned it off. Then he moved a little closer to me on the front seat and said, "Dad, why don't we just talk?" I said, "Son that is a great idea; let's do that."

We talked for a long time. Then, after a bit of silence, he said, "Dad, we like being together, don't we?" It was an electric moment. I don't remember my reply but those words were forever etched in my mind that afternoon. That remains one of the most beautiful moments of my life.

When life is tough, remember beautiful moments and weave them into a good story. Good stories can help people find the courage to face the worst of times.

Some stories are so good they are worth repeating – again and again. Cherish golden moments in your life. Weave them into stories. Share them, more than once, with the people you love. In so doing your little life may be dignified by the joy of helping some hurting person make it through the night. +

CHAPTER 33

How to Make a Difference

Asked what he thought about America these days, a friend said, "We are on our way to hell in a handbasket!"

I have heard that phrase all my life but I have no idea why "hell in a handbasket" implies impending disaster – but it does. My friend did not have to explain that rampant immorality is destroying our culture. I knew what he meant.

If you are a freedom-loving, law-abiding citizen, and you want to do something to stop America's plunge into hell, the best way to do that is to set a good example for others as a decent person who values integrity.

Examples matter. Good examples make a difference. They always have. They always will. The people who are truly "world changers" change the world by their example.

Albert Schweitzer was aware of this. He influenced us all by his example of serving as a missionary doctor among the poor in Africa. And it was Schweitzer who once said, "There is only one way to influence others – and that is by example."

The power of example is extraordinary. Many people become Christians because of the godly example of their parents.

And there are stories of nannies who influenced children more than the children's parents. An example is the nanny of Winston Churchill.

Elizabeth Everest was Churchill's nanny. Churchill said he loved his mother "at a distance," but he adored Mrs. Everest. She taught him the Scriptures. She taught him to pray. She taught him to trust God. In times of trouble as an adult, on the battlefield when his life was in danger, he found himself praying prayers he had learned at his nanny's knee. Throughout his life a picture of Mrs. Everest sat on his desk. When he died her picture lay at his bedside.

So when we applaud Churchill for his courageous example during the Nazi blitz of England, we must also recognize the profound difference that Elizabeth Everest made in the development of Winston's character during his childhood.

The Apostle Paul was a good example for his protégé Timothy. And it is not surprising that as Paul neared the end of his life, he implored Timothy to set a good example as a Christian teacher: "Don't let anyone think less of you because you are young. Be an example to all believers in what you say, in the way you live, in your love, your faith, and your purity." (1 Timothy 4:12, NLT)

Little wonder that Paul urged Timothy to pay close attention to what he was teaching. He knew that what we teach, and the way we live, will encourage others to embrace our Savior or, God forbid, persuade unbelievers to ignore the faith.

Those of us who dare to stand before others and preach the gospel must never forget the haunting words of Edgar Guest:

I'd rather see a sermon than hear one any day; I'd rather one should walk with me than merely tell the way. The eye is a better pupil, more willing than the ear; Fine counsel is confusing, but example is always clear, And the best of all the preachers are the men who live their creeds, For to see a good put in action is what everybody needs.

So here's the moral of this lesson: If you will stay out of the handbasket your good example can help change the world. Your example matters! +

CHAPTER 34

A Little Walk in the Woods

Now and then I need a little walk in the woods. That is good medicine for exhaustion. Constant running drains me even though I enjoy staying busy. Sooner or later I have to turn off the engine and allow my soul to catch up with my body.

Recently I pulled out of the fast lane and found my way to the woods. In a secluded place I took time to enjoy sitting on a log under a large Oak tree. The tree was alive and strong; it was not running, just standing there doing what Oak trees do. It needed no help from me to provide shade for any creatures that chose to enjoy it. The little birds flittering above my head seemed to calm my spirit. Squirrels jumping from limb to limb made me wonder if they ever take time to relax in their nests.

Gentle specks of sunshine filtering through the tree leaves made me feel alive. And a gentle breeze made me wonder why I do not spend more time quietly allowing my inner wheels to stop spinning.

The water of the small pond nearby was peaceful, disturbed only by the two ducks that came near the shore for lunch. They seemed not to notice me as they nervously gulped down seed from tall grass. They are eating too fast, I thought; they'll have indigestion. But I had no right to judge them; my wife says I eat too fast also.

The ground under the tree was sprinkled with dead leaves and acorns. I picked up an acorn and let it teach me. "This big tree was once as small as me," it said. I sat there for a long time thinking about the wonder of it all – that a tiny acorn can become a huge tree. And for that matter a small deed of mercy can become an enormous blessing.

You can worship under a sprawling Oak tree. I did. That tree became something of a sanctuary. While corporate worship is essential, solitary worship can be helpful also. Alone with God you can get in touch with yourself – and you can discover what the Psalmist David meant when he said, "He restores my soul."

I thought about the Psalmist's description of a righteous man: "He shall be like a tree planted by streams of water, which yields its fruit in season and whose leaf does not wither." I am like that Oak tree; its life depends upon the nourishment of the earth and water. I must allow my soul to be nourished by God in order to bear the fruit he expects from my life.

The Prophet Isaiah likens God's people to Oak trees. He describes them this way: "In their righteousness, they will be like great oaks that the Lord has planted for his own glory." I have been blessed by knowing a few men who seemed to me to be "Oaks of righteousness." Would to God that someday I might be known as one.

Under that Oak tree I felt free to talk aloud to God; the squirrels and birds did not seem to mind. I thanked him for my blessings – my wife and family, my friends, the doors he has opened for me, and the years he has given me. I tried to be real. I think he welcomes that.

With the sun slowly setting, and darkness descending, I realized my reflection time had come to an end. I thanked the old tree for its kindness and made my way home. As I walked away I heard God whispering in my heart, "I am glad you enjoyed your walk in the woods, my son. I enjoy restoring your soul and giving you fresh energy for the rest of the journey. We should meet like this more often."

I smiled, thankful for the reminder that my Father loves me, warts and all. The joy of those moments apart lingers still. +

CHAPTER 35

Everybody Needs a Second Chance Sometime

Everybody needs a second chance sometime. We all make mistakes. We all need forgiveness for wrong and sometimes stupid choices.

We all need someone who will not give up on us. Having one such person in your life can be the difference between fulfillment and disaster. A father or a mother can be that person for a son or daughter.

My friend Bob made a lot of wrong choices as a teenager. He ignored the curfew set by his parents, often coming home late at night "drunk as a hoot owl."

Bob's father never responded with anger or chastisement. Instead, no matter how late Bob stayed out at night, he always found his father fully dressed and sitting in a chair waiting for him to come home.

"When I came staggering in Dad never reprimanded me," Bob said. "He simply helped me to bed, always patting me on the back as he said calmly, 'you'll be a fine man one day, son.'"

He was right. Bob finally gave up drinking and, as he said, "turned my life over to God." He went on to college, felt God calling him into the ministry and finished seminary.

Bob understands the gospel. He experienced it. His own father introduced him to the God who never gives up on his children despite their wrong choices. I tremble every time I think about Bob's story. It reveals the true nature of God. He is the God of second chances.

Sin leads to suffering. When we insist on having our own way, defiantly refusing to obey God, we are on the pathway to suffering. None of us gets away with mocking God. He allows us to reap what we sow, to experience the pain of disobedience. When we break covenant with God we suffer the sad consequences of our choices.

Grief accompanies suffering. The Bible tells the story of the Israelites who in exile sat down by the riverside and wept, unable to "sing the Lord's song in a foreign land." Their harps collected dust while they mourned their loss. They only realized how much Jerusalem meant to them after they had lost it.

When the consequences of our wrong choices overwhelm us, we can sit down and weep – or we can learn valuable lessons. When we scoff at the moral laws of God, we are spitting into the wind! We are sliding down the banisters of life with all the splinters pointed at us!

When we break God's commandments we are really breaking ourselves! Would to God that the pain of our sins could teach us that life will work in only one way and that is the way of the Lord!

When we are suffering because of our behavior, nothing can cheer us more than having someone refuse to give up on us. That can be a friend, or a spouse, or a parent, or a colleague at work. Such a person can remind us of the greater reality – that

God never stops loving us! He never gives up on us, even when our sins grieve him.

Wise parents allow their children to suffer the consequences of their behavior, but they never stop loving them. Even when they come in late at night drunk, loving parents will offer them a second chance, and a third, and a fourth, to get it right!

There are many things you can do today but none may be more important than to offer your support to someone who needs a second chance. +

CHAPTER 36

Martin Luther's Portrait a Treasure

Martin Luther was one of the most colorful characters in church history. Besides spearheading the Protestant Reformation Luther lived a fascinating life as a priest and theology professor. Had I lived 500 years ago in Germany I would have loved teaming up with Luther.

A portrait of Luther hangs on the wall in my office, a gift from my good friend John Wertz, a longtime Lutheran pastor. I treasure that portrait because of the kindness of my Lutheran friend and my admiration for the remarkable life Luther lived. While the likeness of John Wesley also adorns my office wall, I have enjoyed learning in recent years Luther's interesting views on many subjects.

When, for example, an admiring woman told Luther she hoped he could live another forty years, he replied, "God forbid!" He said he did not wish to live much longer mainly because the world was "full of nothing but devils." He had no use for physicians and insisted that "in God's name" he would eat "whatever tastes good to me." While I do not share Luther's disdain for doctors, I share his enormous desire to "eat whatever tastes good to me."

For many years Luther condemned vows of celibacy for priests. But in late November 1524 Luther wrote to a friend, "I shall never take a wife." Six months later he married a former nun who bore him six children. While Luther was busy preaching and writing his wife Katharina helped earn a living by farming the land and taking in boarders.

Luther was a very practical man. If water, for example, was not available for a baptism, beer would serve just as well. During a time of drought Luther prayed earnestly for rain. And that very night some rain fell. When he was a young man games with cards and dice were forbidden. In later years he embraced such games as good exercise for the mind.

Luther scolded preachers for their scholarly sermons on lofty themes. He advised them to be simple and direct in preaching so that they could be understood by young people and children. As for the "learned doctors," if they do not want to listen, "they can leave." Luther once observed that "there are many fluent preachers who speak at length but say nothing, who have words without substance." Sadly, such preachers were not limited to the days of Luther.

Not everything about Luther was admirable. The German reformer had no patience with atheists. Once he was asked about a citizen of Wittenberg who confessed publicly that he had not received communion for 15 years. Luther said that after a couple of admonitions he would declare the man excommunicated and to be "treated like a dog." He went on to say, "If the unbeliever dies in this condition, let him be buried in the carrion pit like a dog."

Luther was asked about a man who felt called to preach but whose wife had a haughty spirit and did not want to have a parson for a husband. What should the man do? Luther replied, "If she were my wife I'd say to her, 'Will you go with me?' Say quickly, No or Yes.' If she said No, I would at once take another wife and leave her."

When asked if a priest should give the sacrament to a man he knew to be a liar, Luther replied, "Do what Christ did; he gave the sacrament to the betrayer Judas."

One man asked Luther about where God was before the creation of the world. Luther quoted Augustine whose answer to the question had been, "God was making hell for those who are inquisitive."

Luther had a way of saying things that were not always polite and spiritual. The forgiveness of his sins was terribly important to Luther. Good old boys could understand him well when he observed: "Apart from the forgiveness of sins I can't stand a bad conscience at all; the devil hounds me about a single sin until the world becomes too small for me, and afterward I feel like spitting on myself for having been afraid of such a small thing." Some of us have shared that feeling at times.

Luther and his wife struggled in their marriage like most couples do. But he found great joy in his marriage. I found myself saying Amen to this tender observation by the reformer: "There is no sweeter union than that in a good marriage. Nor is there any death more bitter than that which separates a married couple. Only the deaths of children come close to this; how much this hurts I have myself experienced." Luther and his wife lost their daughter Elizabeth in her first year.

Martin had a delightful sense of humor. One evening he attended a wedding. Before the evening meal he advised the bridegroom to be content with the general custom and "be lord in his house whenever his wife is not at home!"

Luther endured poor health in his later years but was able to continue preaching. He preached his last sermon three days before his death in 1546 at age 62. Aware that Luther was dying during his last night on earth, Luther's two companions shouted to him: "Reverend Father, are you ready to die trusting in your Lord Jesus Christ and to confess the doctrine which you have taught in his name?" Luther replied "Yes" and died a few minutes later.

Salvation, Luther believed, is not earned by good deeds but is received only as the free gift of God's grace through faith in Jesus Christ. That remains to this day a cardinal belief of Protestants, all of whom are indebted to Martin Luther for his life and his teaching.

When I glance at Luther's portrait on my office wall I thank God for what that man's courage and conviction means to all who believe in the priesthood of all believers. +

CHAPTER 37

Helping People See God

I read somewhere about a young man who was desperately seeking God. He sought out a wise old man who lived nearby and asked him: "Old man, how I can I see God?"

The old man, who must have known God at a depth few people ever experience, pondered the question. Then he responded gently: "Young man, I am not sure that I can help you – for you see, I have a very different problem. I cannot not see him."

The old man's answer makes me wonder what I might have said had I been that old man. I think I might have said, "Young man, I see God everywhere." And if he had asked me to explain, I would have begun with his question.

I see God in the heart's quest to see God. Only God could have put in our hearts the longing to see God. Every reasonable person longs to know that there is a benevolent God responsible for creation. So in a sense the young man's question is the question of every human being. Is God real? If so, how can I see God?

I have been a minister for 65 years. What is ministry? It is more than preaching. It is more than pastoral care and more than growing and maintaining churches. Ministry is helping people to see God, and seeing him, to get to know him, then love and serve him. So where can one see God?

I see God in the Bible. What a great book it is. It shows me Jesus and tells me that when I see Jesus, I have seen God. Jesus puts a face on God. Before the birth of Jesus, no one had seen God. God had made himself known by giving us laws to live by. But then God chose to send his son into the world and that son, the Bible tells us, is the image of the invisible God. Only a loving God could have inspired the creation of so great a book as the Holy Bible!

I see God in the kindness and forgiving love of my wife. For 64 years she has constantly offered me compassion instead of criticism for my many mistakes as a husband. Her kindness has been like a magnet drawing me toward a more excellent way to live. Only a loving God could have produced such a woman!

I see God in the frequent telephone calls of my friend George Mathison. When my phone rings at 5:30 in the morning I figure it is George calling. When I answer, George says, "Brother Walter, I have been on my knees praying for you this morning and I just wanted to call and tell you how much I love you." Only a loving God could produce a man like George!

I see God in the star in an apple. Many times my wife has cut an apple open before children and shown them the remarkable star in the center of the apple. I see God as I observe the awe in the eyes of little children. Only a loving God could have thought to put a star in the center of an apple!

I see God in the healing of hearts torn asunder by bitterness and despair. My friend Billy Gaither's parents divorced when he was ten years old. He prayed earnestly, asking God to fix his broken family.

When God did not answer, and his parents were not reconciled, Billy was angry with God. He felt unloved, unwanted and desperate. He quit praying, feeling that God did not care about him. Six years later Billy was invited to join a youth group in church. Through other youth and a caring pastor, Billy felt God saying to him, "Welcome back. I missed you." Only a loving God could restore the joy of a young man whose life had been shattered by the divorce of his parents!

I see God in the Knock Out Rose bushes in our yard. No matter the season they keep on blooming, offering beautiful new blooms every five to six weeks. Only a loving God could have shown Rose Breeder Bill Radler how to produce such an amazing rose bush!

I see God in the faces of the people with whom I worship. As we praise God together I see people come alive with new energy to face the challenges of everyday life. Only a loving God could turn worship into a life-giving renewal of faith, hope and love!

Yes, I see God everywhere – in every breath I take, in every step I take, in every morsel of food I eat, in the sun and the moon and the stars that brighten the night sky. Only a loving God could create such a beautiful world!

If you have trouble seeing him, please look again. He is everywhere, waiting to startle you with the reality of his loving Presence! +

CHAPTER 38

Enduring Greenhorn Preachers

A greenhorn is an awkward and inexperienced person. That word fit me perfectly when I began preaching. How people endured my preaching back then remains a mystery.

Methodists usually start greenhorn preachers in small country churches. These churches are the training ground for new preachers. After some years I figured out why greenhorns are given a circuit of several small churches. Most of them only have worship services once or twice a month so the people are spared the pain of listening to poor preaching every Sunday.

A greenhorn at age 21, I became the pastor of four small churches near Milstead, Alabama. I had no training. I knew nothing about how to prepare or preach a sermon. But the people seemed to like me from the start, probably because my first sermons were no more than ten to 15 minutes long.

The Methodist hierarchy, after asking me to read and report on four books, had issued me a license to preach. While a student at Auburn University I was appointed by Dr. W. F. Calhoun, superintendent of the Montgomery District, to serve the LaPlace Circuit at a salary of $1900 a year. They provided a parsonage and allowed me to continue my studies at Auburn.

The good people of those churches were not surprised that I was a babe in the woods. All their pastors for many years had been student pastors. I was expected me to learn on the job.

My learning was not without its embarrassing moments. One of my churches was the old LaPlace Church, one of the earliest Methodist churches organized in Alabama. The church was just off Highway 80 in Shorter, now the home of VictoryLand Greyhound Park and gambling center. On a good Sunday 30 to 40 people showed up for worship at the LaPlace Church.

One faithful worshiper was Wright Noble. He appeared to be a pillar of the church so I decided one Sunday to ask him to pray. I figured I could use some help since I was not comfortable praying or preaching.

I learned that day never to call on someone to pray in church without asking permission beforehand. From the pulpit, I asked politely, "Mr. Noble, will you lead us in prayer?"

Without a moment's hesitation, he stood up and replied in a strong, firm voice, "I beg to be excused; that's what we pay the preacher for!"

Embarrassed, I stumbled through a prayer while most of my parishioners were quietly chuckling. I have no doubt Mr. Noble was a Christian. I am sure he was a praying man. However, I never heard him pray.

Thus did my training for pastoral work begin. Mr. Noble and others like him made sure that I understood why they paid my salary. There were certain things I was expected to do, none of which was ever explained to me in a "job description." They were quite willing to teach me my duties in one embarrassing moment after another.

People pay the preacher for many reasons. Some pay him to mind his own business, which does not include "running the church." The explanation was plain and simple: "You stick to preaching and we will run the church."

In one church I asked the church treasurer for a report on the offerings. He said, "We are fine, preacher, just fine." I asked, "Do you make a monthly report to the Board?" He replied, "No, I just let everybody know if we get behind. Right now, everything is fine." I think he kept the church's money in a cigar box, but I never found out. He taught me that it was none of my business how much money the church had collected.

Speaking of money, I think most preachers feel like I do about being paid. I was amazed that I could be paid to have such a great job. Our work is not drudgery and we are not in the ministry for the money. Some of us feel that we are paid far more than we deserve. And some of our parishioners agree!

A retired preacher was asked by a senior pastor to join his staff as the minister of visitation, to care for the sick and homebound.

He replied, "You don't have enough money to hire me to visit the hospitals. When I was a pastor, the church paid me my full salary to visit the sick; I preached for free!"

I think his attitude was unique. I always felt it was a high privilege to minister to the sick and develop strong relationships with people who were hurting and anxious.

A preacher gets paid to do many things. People have a thousand expectations of their preacher. Some people feel like they are not getting their money's worth; others wish they could pay the pastor more.

In a healthy church the preacher and the people work together as a team, shepherding people with love. Key leaders trust their pastor and realize that he needs their help; he or she cannot do everything alone. Teamwork is essential.

Over many years I have had the joy of sharing ministry with some tremendous lay people who were servants of Christ. They were in my balcony pulling for me and praying for me. My gratitude for those teammates is boundless.

But my most profound gratitude is for the dear country saints who tolerated this greenhorn when I knew nothing and lovingly encouraged me to believe that I could learn how to do the work of a pastor. I am forever in their debt. +

CHAPTER 39

Sharing Memories Strengthens Your Mind

One good way to strengthen your mind is to share your memories. Before you can share them you must collect them. I find it fun to recall and refine memories of my childhood, then share them with my children, grandchildren and great grandchildren – and sometimes with good friends who have stored precious memories like my own.

Since our family lived in the country I rode a big yellow bus to school from grade one through grade twelve. But by the time I was in grade eleven I was driving the bus. I still find it hard to believe the school system trusted a 17-year-old boy to drive a school bus. Fortunately, I did not have an accident.

Nearly all of the roads were gravel roads when I began school in 1938. And not all of them were paved when I was a senior. The ride to school took about an hour during which we choked on a tortuous blend of dust and hot air.

As I learned to read I fell in love with books. My mother had exposed me to a few books but at school I discovered that marvelous room called the library. To break the monotony of the long bus rides I got in the habit of reading books I had checked out of the library. The adventures of Tarzan and the Rover Boys were favorites. How I managed to read while bouncing over pot holes and breathing that dust I will never know. But it helped to pass the time.

When I was a fifth grader I persuaded the bus driver to do something he would not be allowed to do today. At one point the driver turned off the main road and traveled some five miles until the road ended. There he would pick up or unload some children, then turn around and retrace his route.

Most days the driver allowed me, James and Tom to get off the bus so we could play in the sand by the side of the road until he returned ten to fifteen minutes later. That was high adventure. It never dawned on me that the driver might be a little nervous until we got back on the bus. It was exhilarating to get off the bus and show the other kids what courage we had. For a few minutes we were real men.

About two hundred yards behind our home was a swimming hole in a narrow creek. In the summertime my cousins and I would strip off our clothes, splash the water to scare the snakes away and enjoy a break from the heat. In later years I shuddered to think about the risks we took, playing so carelessly around Cottonmouth Water Moccasins. But back then we were young, naïve and carefree. We never gave any thought to danger or dying.

When I was young that swimming hole was huge. To swim across to the other side was quite a challenge. Since those days I have gone back to that old swimming hole and laughed to discover that the distance to the other side of the creek is only about 12 feet. Memories have a way of playing tricks on our minds.

Daddy's farm included some rich river bottom land that bordered the Tallapoosa River for a few miles. As a young man I loved to roam and hunt in the thick woods along the river. There were places that were special – places few people knew about -- where I could pick and enjoy sweet Scuppernongs, play on sand bars and skip rocks across the river's surface, or just sit and think. I enjoyed the special sounds of the woods, birds chirping and squirrels scampering, while sitting alone on a log and pondering the meaning of life.

Scuppernongs in the woods were a delicacy free for the taking. I savored the sweet juice, spitting the hulls on the ground. Sometimes I would go back with a bucket and pick enough for Mama to make a few pints of jelly.

My kids find it hard to believe that at night we would sit on the front porch, catch lightning bugs, tell ghost stories or play Red Rover. We had time to relax and enjoy being together because we were not plagued with cell phones or televisions. Life was more simple back then.

Reliving pleasant memories cures boredom and is good exercise for the mind. It is best to forget the bad stuff and focus on precious memories. Life is too short to give much time to the stuff that can breed resentment or despair.

The mind has a marvelous capacity to remember so collect your memories. Have fun sharing them with others. The older you get, the more you will need a strong mind to help you finish strong. +

CHAPTER 40

God Still Sends People Out

Recently our church called seven men and women to the altar. We laid hands on them and commissioned them to go to Africa. Their mission was to share the love of Jesus with the people of Siansowa Village in the southern region of Zambia. The team came back fired up and eager to motivate our congregation to find creative ways to partner with the three thousand people in that poor village.

This act of "sending forth" people in the name of Jesus reminded me of a story Doctor Luke tells in the Acts of the Apostles. The disciples in the little church in Antioch were worshiping and fasting when they heard the Holy Spirit say, "Set apart for me Barnabas and Saul for the work to which I have called them."

This was the first missionary journey of Barnabas and Paul. The two of them, having found new life in Christ, were sent to tell others the good news of salvation. Luke says that, "after fasting and praying," the church elders "laid their hands on them and sent them off."

While Barnabas and Paul were sent out by their fellow disciples in the church at Antioch, Luke emphasizes that they were actually "sent out by the Holy Spirit." The Spirit called them. The Spirit equipped them. The Spirit sent them out. But the Spirit sent them through the church with the encouragement and prayers of the church.

It is interesting that the Holy Spirit spoke to the disciples while they were "worshiping the Lord and fasting." The focus of their worship was "the Lord," Jesus Christ. It was not on butterflies and caterpillars or the birds and the bees. While the beauty of nature is a precious gift of God, Christian worship must always be centered in the greatest gift – His Son Jesus Christ. The life, ministry, crucifixion and resurrection of Jesus constitute the inexhaustible subject of authentic worship.

In the Antioch church fasting is connected to worship. Though fasting is not commanded by the New Testament, Christians have found that fasting helps them discern the will of God. Jesus fasted. The early disciples fasted. Christians through the ages have fasted.

We need not assume that the words of the Holy Spirit were audible. When the Spirit "said" to the worshipers, "Set apart for me Barnabas and Saul for the work to which I have called them," we may assume they heard the Spirit's voice as we do – in their minds and hearts. However the Spirit spoke, his command was persuasive. The worshipers were moved to fast and pray, then obey the Spirit.

The definition of the word "holy" is to be "set apart," as in set apart for the work of God. All Christians are called to be holy, set apart for the work of Christ. It was not the "laying on of hands" that empowered Barnabas and Paul for their mission. Then and today the laying on of hands is simply a traditional practice of inviting the Spirit to fill the recipients with the grace to do the will of God. The power belongs to the Spirit, not to the hands of those praying.

Thriving churches still "send forth disciples" into their communities – and across the world. Weak and dying churches set up camp and invite people to come to them. They invite but do not send. The attitude, "We are here if you need us," will do little to win the world to Christ.

Clearly the church today needs to find new ways to send out believers to share the gospel with their neighbors. We have all received the mandate to "be his witnesses" and to "go into all the world." The Great Commission applies to all believers, not a select few.

The Lord's command, "Go and make disciples of all nations," applies to us all. Unfortunately, some of us have perceived this as the Lord's instructions to missionaries, not ordinary disciples. We need to re-think this passage. Some commentators suggest that the Lord was actually saying, "As you go about, living your daily life, do your best to make disciples of everyone you meet." And that is a command, not a suggestion, to all believers!

Instead of saying to worshipers as they leave church, "Depart in peace," we could say, "Go forth as disciples sent out to share the good news of Christ in the place where you work, in your neighborhood, in your school and in all the places where your witness can make a difference."

The Spirit who sent out Barnabas and Paul can send us out and release in us the same power that birthed the church in the first century. +

CHAPTER 41

The Sweet Pagan Embroidery of Easter

Though Easter is a Christian holy day it has been embar-
rassingly commercialized. The observance of Easter
is rife with pagan concepts. And while Easter Sunday is
celebrated by millions of Christians across the world, the
word "Easter" is not in the Bible.

The word is derived from the name of an ancient pagan god-
dess of spring. And for people who are not followers of Christ,
"Easter" is merely an adjective describing things that have nothing
to do with the resurrection of Jesus Christ.

We speak, for example, of Easter shoes. Growing up, my siblings and I sometimes got a new pair of shoes to wear on Easter
Sunday. It was a family custom made possible by our friends Sears
& Roebuck. If the farming had been good the year before, Mama
might get a new hat and the children a new outfit. But shoes and
clothes have nothing to do with the true meaning of Easter.

Rabbits are an appendage to Easter. As Easter nears the
stores are full of bunny rabbits of all sizes. Huge bunnies attract

customers. Children pester their parents to buy them a live rabbit but settle for a chocolate bunny. As a young boy I raised rabbits. A pair soon became a dozen. But I soon tired of caring for the rabbits so we enjoyed fried rabbit for supper.

This secularization of Easter is so extensive that we have Easter eggs, Easter baskets, Easter lilies and Easter sales. Many churches sponsor Easter egg hunts for the children though often no mention is made of the resurrection. Easter eggs are pretty. Children have fun hunting them. The key is fun.

Though an egg hunt may be fun, for large churches it can be a big production. One church "hides" three thousand Easter eggs annually. One tired but loyal volunteer remarked, "Two hundred of those eggs will never be found by the children; we will uncover them weeks later while tending to the lawn." This raises the question as to how much of this Easter madness the church should baptize.

Florists love Easter. They sell thousands of Easter lilies. Some churches make a profit adorning the chancel area with lilies. Buy them for five dollars apiece, sell them for ten and clear five dollars for a missionary project.

Easter lilies have sentimental value for me. When I was born in the spring, my dad picked some wild Easter lilies in the woods behind our house. He put them in a Mason jar beside my crib. Wild lilies still grow behind the old home place.

Easter occurs in the spring because the death and resurrection of Jesus happened in springtime, at the time of the annual Jewish Passover. So we associate Easter with the budding of flowers, the new life of nature.

Spring is a delightful season. Winter is past and the earth is bursting with the beauty of green leaves, spring flowers and budding trees. New life is everywhere as what appeared dead comes suddenly to life. But what happened to Jesus on Easter morning was much more than the changing cycles of nature.

His resurrection was not like the spring birth of flowers. His resurrection was qualitatively different. Flowers born in spring will die. Next spring new flowers may come from the seed or bulbs that have lain dormant in winter. But as much as we delight in the beauty of spring, this process of nature is not what the Bible means by the resurrection of the dead.

The dead body of Jesus did not "sprout" buds from which a new person grew. God infused life into his dead body and he was physically alive again. God transformed his old body into a new glorified body. The tomb was not opened so Jesus could get out; it was opened so the women and the disciples could see that the tomb was empty. The Risen Christ had conquered death! The grave could not hold him!

Lovely flowers and colorful butterflies are wonderful gifts of God. We can enjoy their beauty and embrace them as expressions of God's love. We can enjoy a chocolate bunny. The kids can hunt eggs. Buy the children some new shoes – if they need them. But do all this without including these Easter parasites in the same breath with the resurrection of Jesus. Butterflies and bunny rabbits cannot save us from our sins!

Cynics say that the grave is the end. Beyond the death of the human body, there is nothing more, only dust. The resurrection of Jesus was God's answer to hopeless cynicism. It was God's way of saying, "Don't be afraid. There is more! So much more that you can hardly imagine the wonderful eternal life I have planned for you - if you will trust my Son for salvation!"

Enjoy the wonders of bulbs, seeds and cocoons. Celebrate the coming of spring. But remember that the resurrection of Jesus has done something for you that bunnies and butterflies can never do. His resurrection has opened the gates of heaven and offers you blessed hope that you will see your loved ones again.

This is the faith God's people enjoy when the true meaning of the resurrection is divested of all the sweet pagan embroidery. That is why our churches are crowded on Easter Sunday. People are looking for hope! They are looking for a family that will love them and give them reason to believe there is life beyond the grave. Let us welcome them warmly and invite them to embrace with us the good news that Easter is God's gift of hope. +

CHAPTER 42

When You Don't Know
What to Do

There hangs in our bedroom a framed statement cro-
cheted by my mother. It reads: "Marriage – May there
be such a oneness between you that when one weeps the
other will taste salt."

I have mulled over that message many times since Dean and
I were married more than 64 years ago. The idea of tasting the salt
of each other's tears is a powerful reminder of what it means to be
joined together in holy wedlock.

I have indeed tasted the salt of her tears. It happens when
two have become one and the trials of life descend like a whirl-
wind. When Dean was crying because of the excruciating pain of
a herniated disc in her back, I found myself kissing away her tears.
It dawned on me that I was once again tasting salt, the salt of her
tears.

During the hours when she was struggling with the pain in
her back, I was also trying to get ready to preach the following
Sunday. I was grieving for Dean but also pondering the meaning
of the scripture I had chosen for my sermon. That has been the

pattern of my life – wading through the common struggles of life while devising a sermon for the coming Sunday. It must be God's way of helping us who preach to see firsthand how the Gospel speaks to the real problems people face every day. I know it has helped me preach with greater relevancy and understanding.

So, while Dean was enduring severe back pain, and unaware of all my thoughts, I was pondering a dilemma faced by King Jehoshaphat hundreds of years ago. I was fearful about Dean's back and the King was gripped with fear for his people. I was struck by how fear brought both the King and me to the same conclusion. The King said in despair, "We don't know what to do."

I did not know what to do either! I wanted to help my beloved wife but did not know how to help her. But in those agonizing hours I did the same thing that King Jehoshaphat did: I turned to God for help. And both the King and I found the help we needed by turning to God.

There is a great lesson in this story of a King who did not know what to do. Let me briefly recap the story. Jehoshaphat was King of Israel for 25 years about 850 years before Christ. He had an army of a million soldiers. But on one occasion several enemy nations banded together and made war on Israel. The king was told that a vast army was on its way to fight them.

Jehoshaphat knew he was outmanned. So he turned to God and called on the nation of Judah to turn to God. They gathered to pray for God's help. The king stood and prayed before the people, concluding his prayer by saying, "We don't know what to do but we are looking to you, our eyes are on you."

When the king was finished, a man named Jahaziel stood up. He was moved by the Spirit to speak. He addressed the king and the crowd and said, "Listen, don't be afraid or discouraged because of this vast army. The battle is not yours but God's. And he will be with you!"

After Jahaziel spoke, the king and all the people bowed with their faces to the ground and began to worship the Lord. Some of the Levites began to praise the Lord with a very loud voice! The king was so encouraged that he appointed a choir to begin singing and praising God. The choir went out before the army singing, "Give thanks to the Lord, for his love endures forever." The scripture says that as they began to sing and praise, the Lord began to work and soon victory was theirs.

This story offers us some great principles to remember when we don't know what to do: 1. To turn to God is to start praying! 2. To turn to God is to remember that God cares! 3. To turn to God is to realize that He is with us and he is able to move by his Spirit ordinary people to give us hope! Jehaziel was such a man! 4. To turn to God in these days is to turn our eyes upon Jesus! 5. To turn to Jesus is to realize that because He is with us we have hope of victory no matter what we are facing!

So what is the point of this convoluting story of a wife's back pain and an Israelite King? The point is quite simple: The next time you don't know what to do, kiss your wife and turn to God. While you are tasting salt, He will help you. +

CHAPTER 43

Go Get Bill

Bill Hinson was a Methodist preacher, a good one, one of the best really. He followed Charles Allen at First Methodist in Houston, Texas, and had a long and fruitful ministry at that great church.

On the Sunday in 1983 when Charles Allen introduced Bill as the new pastor, Bill won the hearts of the people in his opening remarks. He told of riding in an elevator a few days before with a man who kept looking at him and finally, bluntly, said, "Are you the one who is going to First Church, Houston?"

Bill said he answered, "I am." After that there was an awkward silence. Bill said, "He kept looking me up and down. I wanted to be taller, I wanted to grow at least a foot or more. I couldn't. Finally, the ride was so long and the silence so awkward I said, to break the silence, 'Pray for me.' The man said, as he shook his head, 'I am. You're going to need it.'"

A powerful preacher but a humble man, Bill knew how to laugh at himself and get others to laugh with him. He served First Church for 18 years, retired at age 65, and died a few years later at his home near Huntsville, Alabama.

Bill began preaching in his teens in country churches in south Georgia. He enjoyed telling the story of a little boy who heard him preach his second sermon. On the front pew of a little country church the boy sat waving his dirty feet to and fro, until Bill, mesmerized by the boy, gave up trying to preach and stumbled through the benediction. The boy came up to Bill and said, "Brother Bill, would you come home with me and have lunch at our house?" Bill agreed, met his family, enjoyed a meal with them, and went back to South Georgia College where he was a student and forgot about the boy.

A couple of weeks later Bill got a letter in his college mailbox. In the envelope was fifty-seven cents in pennies, nickels and dimes. A letter from that little boy, ten years old, said, "Dear Brother Bill, I'm sending you my egg money to help you go to school to learn to be a better preacher."

Bill laughed and then called the boy's father and told him he wanted to send the money back. The boy's father said, "You can't. He's sending you every penny of his profits. He never took better care of those chickens in his life. He's going to keep on sending you his profit and if you send it back you'll break his heart." Bill said another letter came the next week, and continued to come for months "and the months became years."

Bill said, "There came a time when I didn't laugh anymore, but I'd get his letter and I'd go back to my room and get on my knees and say, 'Oh God, help me to be worthy of that little boy's sacrifice." Bill began to apply himself to his studies with greater determination to do his best.

Bill was a senior in seminary when his daddy died. After having a stroke and a heart attack, Bill's daddy seemed to be im His little sister was the only family member present in the room when his daddy's chest pains began. When the pains began, Bill's daddy raised the hand not immobilized by his stroke and said to his daughter, "Go get Bill and ask him to hold my hand and help the hurt." She explained that Bill was 200 miles away but ran to get the doctor. The doctor was unable to save him.

Unable to get home before his daddy died, Bill wrecked his car trying. When he arrived his sister told him about his daddy's request to go get Bill so he could hold his hand and help the hurt.

Overwhelmed by a feeling of self-pity, Bill said, "Oh God, I would have given ten years of my life to have made it here in time to hold that hand!"

In the months that followed Bill said he began to realize that as long as he lived "there will be people all around me holding up their hands asking me to hold them and to help the hurt. And I had to decide whether I was going to go through life holding hands with myself or reaching out to help the hurt of the world."

As I read Bill's story I kept hearing Bill's daddy crying out in pain, saying "Go get Bill." Those three words keep bouncing around in my brain: "Go get Bill; Go get Bill." Finally I got on my knees and said, "Oh God, help me as long as I live to be available to anyone who cries, 'Go get Walter.'"

Like Bill Hinson, each of us has to decide whether to go through life holding our own hands or holding the hands of hurting people who need us. +

CHAPTER 44

The Remarkable Power of Encouraging Words

Words have enormous power. Critical words can destroy our hope. Encouraging words can energize us to succeed. History is filled with proof of this premise.

Benjamin West was an incredibly gifted painted. Born in Springfield, Pennsylvania in 1738, West had little formal education and could hardly spell but he could paint remarkable portraits. He became a close friend of Benjamin Franklin and painted Franklin's portrait.

West loved to tell the story of his first attempt to paint. One day when he was a young boy, and his mother was not home, he decided he would paint a picture of his sister. Soon, working with bottles of ink and paper, he had made what he described as "an awful mess."

When his mother returned and saw the mess her son had made, she was very wise. She chose not to scold the boy. Instead she picked up the poor painting, studied it for a moment, and said to Benjamin, "What a beautiful picture of your sister!" Then, cupping his face in her hands, she kissed him. Years later, whenever

Benjamin West told that story, he always said, "With that kiss I became a painter."

I hate stories like that. They remind me of the many times I blew it as a father. Viewing the mess one of my sons had made, I would so often say with a frown on my face, "Look what a mess you have made!" West's story reminds me of opportunities I had to offer words of affirmation rather than criticism.

History books are full of inspiring stories, such as one about American author Nathaniel Hawthorne. After losing his job working for the government in the customs house, Hawthorne went home in despair. Full of self-pity, he moaned and groaned to his wife about how he had been mistreated. After listening patiently for a while, his wife got up, found a pen and ink, put it on the table and lit a fire. Then, putting her arms around her husband's shoulders, she said firmly, "Now you can write your novel!"

Hawthorne was so inspired by his wife's encouragement that he did just that. Soon the world was blessed by the novel he titled The Scarlet Letter, a book of fiction that remains an American classic.

When I first read this story about Hawthorne, I thought, "Hey, I am married to a woman like Nathaniel's wife!" And I am! Repeatedly, when I have succumbed to despair, instead of criticizing me she has said firmly, "Get up big boy; pick up the pieces and let's get moving!" Like Hawthorne's wife she has refused to let me grovel in gloom and defeat. And like Hawthorne, I am a blessed man because of her choice of words.

Positive words help people. Negative words can destroy people. Think about what it means to you to be around people who know how and when to pat you on the back and say "Well done!" And consider how little it has helped you to be around people who are constantly saying, "You could have done better!"

Speaking to a large group of prison inmates, Evangelist Bill Glass asked, "How many of you had parents who told you that you would end up in prison one day?" Almost every hand went up. Negative words have devastating influence. A friend of mine is still haunted by the chilling, angry words his father said to him many times, "You will never amount to anything!"

The next time you are tempted to complain about the mess someone has made, count to ten before you speak and try to remember the remarkable power of encouraging words. You may do more than make someone's day; you may make someone's life.

+ + +